THE FINALISTS

EDITED BY JENNI HARRISON

First published in Great Britain in 2017 by:

Forward Poetry
Coltsfoot Drive
Peterborough
PE2 9BF
Telephone: 01733 890099
Website: www.forwardpoetry.co.uk

FOREWORD

In 2009, Poetry Rivals was launched. It was one of the biggest and most prestigious competitions ever held by Forward Poetry. Due to the popularity and success of this talent contest like no other, we have taken Poetry Rivals into 2016, where it has proven to be even bigger and better
than previous years.

Poets of all ages and from all corners of the globe were invited to write a poem that demonstrated true creative talent - a poem that would stand out from the rest. We are proud to present the resulting anthology, an inspiring collection of verse carefully selected by our team of editors. Reflecting the vibrancy of the modern poetic world, it is brimming with imagination and diversity.

As well as encouraging creative expression, Poetry Rivals has also given writers young and old a vital opportunity to showcase their work to the public, thus providing it with the wider audience it so richly deserves.

CONTENTS

THE
POEMS

Her

With each step you take, is another reason why you are the one I want to be with you. Each step you take on the earth, brings out the beauty around, knowing that there is an angel with a halo shining brightly in front of them. As you inhale with your eyes close and exhale with your eyes open, the sight of this gets me on my toes to see an angel breath in the air in which I breathe in too. Too nervous to approach you.

Too nervous to call you. Too nervous to do anything. All I can do is watch you. Watch you as you bless the earth with the sight of yourself. Looking at your body, it's like someone create and shaped your body into the perfect shape, I see before me. What can I do? Just look? No. Action should be taken but the fear in me won't let me.

I can only look at you from an distance for now until I have the courage to walk up to you and tell you how I feel but when will this be? Tomorrow? Next week? Next month? Next year? I don't know. You've taken over my mind, with the thought of having you laying next to me. The pain of hiding my feelings in the shadows is too much. It's time to open up to you and tell you how I feel or I may never get the chance again.

Here it is. I love you and I want to be with you. You've given me feelings I have never felt before. Seeing you leaves me speechless and confused to think I could have ever the chance to be with you. I don't know how a guy like me could be with an angel like you but, I can't hide no longer. I've come out of the shadows for you. For once, I'm doing something for me and this is something I want. I want you. I don't know what else to say but I love you again.

Danial Zabir

My Sweet Tara

Since the moment you were taken I have not stopped thinking
about you,
Not that before you were gone, you were ever far from my mind;
You were my sweet newborn, with virgin-soft skin and bright blue
eyes,
I was so lucky to have been granted you,
And I watched you grow,
Your hair becoming uncontrollable tangles,
And those newborn blues turning to the same muddy brown as my
own;
It was my job, the job of any parent, to protect you,
And for nineteen years, Tara, I did my best;
I was so proud of you,
Becoming a great big sister,
Not straying far from the path you were born on,
Even becoming the first of our family to go to college,
College was difficult for your father and me,
As we'd never had you so far away,
Our family was still close though,
Because you would call us every day;
Then your first year was over
And you came back for the summer,
Cluttering our living room with your things,
Everyone was so happy to see you,
Your little sister probably the most,
Every day she spoke of you,
You had a relationship that was unbelievably close;
Coming home, you'd began a new hobby,
You cycled, for hours it seemed,

Through the woods that surrounded our home,
To places where your father and I had never been,
But when you reached you destination, Tara,
You were too tired for the trip back,
So I would drive to collect you,
And we'd meet as you walked along the side track;
Then, one time, beginning like any other,
I came to meet you but you weren't there,
So I drove back and forth between home and where you said
you'd be
But I couldn't find you and I began to panic;
I had lost my baby in the crowd.
You had vanished into thin air,
Suddenly snatched up
As though God himself had reached down and taken you;
A friend had to pick up your sister from her sleepover
And I continued to search,
Back and forth along the roads as your father called the police;
They quickly set up a team to look,
And your family and friends and I tried to pitch in
But shock had taken over and the end was beginning,
Because the police told us you'd most likely been taken,
And witnesses had seen a pick-up truck following close behind
you,
Then the police found your cassette player off the side of the road
And I knew that was you trying to lead us;
Then a month had gone by and nothing new came up,
Our living room was still cluttered with all your stuff,
Summer had ended and school had begun,
Then snow fell over the forest and I couldn't bear to think of you
out in it alone,

My sweet, Tara, wandering through the woods
Trying desperately to find your way home;
I decided many nights to stay up for you, just in case,
Many times I'd see the sun come up and I'd still be awake;
Then suddenly a whole year had slipped by,
And every day I am told that the chances of you being alive are
slim to none,
But I still hope you are alive and one day you'll come back home;
It's affected your sister more than I could imagine,
But she tries *desperately* to hide it,
She wants to be strong for me,
Because you being gone has really broken every piece I have;
Two years gone and the police officially move on from the case
With another missing persons to chase,
That's fine though because I still go out and look,
I have visions of you cycling towards me,
Then you disappear as quickly as you appeared,
And I realise, every time, that I would give *anything* to have you
here;
Time adds up and suddenly ten years go by,
Nothing that'll lead us to you surfaces,
Just a photograph and theories based on lies,
Your dad passes away, and it breaks my heart to know,
That you weren't around to say what he so *desperately* wanted to
hear,
And that was your voice, for just one more time,
Sweet Tara, I've given up hope for you to be fine;
But I still stay awake, just in case,
Just in case they let you go,
And you come home to see me still awake, having never given up
hope,
But you don't,

And I am told to move on,
But how do you move on when there are so many unanswered
questions,
And a child that's just gone;
I've taken a big step though, by packing away your stuff,
And it surprises me to see my living room look so clean
When, for ten years, it's housed my last few pieces of you;
By the fifteen-year mark I decide enough is enough,
I can't bear living in our home anymore,
Everything reminds me of you and it's too tough to get through,
So I move to be away,
But not a day goes by where you do not dominate my mind;
The 20-year anniversary is a chilling affair,
Your little sister brings her kids with her,
And I realise that she has outgrown you in every way possible,
And that *I still feel* that heavy despair that began the day that you
were gone;
We toast to you, to your soul in Heaven,
And beg the lord to let us find your remains,
Because you are dead, I've come to accept that,
But I need the closure only a funeral can bring;
It's been 22 years and my health has deteriorated,
I am dying, surrounded by the people I love
And I feel guilt because you didn't get that same grace,
As I take one of the last few of my remaining breaths,
I only think of you, my sweet Tara,
And I envision you waiting for me beyond the veil,
Then, for the briefest of moments,
I think of the person who took you,
And curse his soul to Hell,

As the parent of a missing child,
He has granted access to the most exclusive club in the world,
And it's the one club I don't want to be in.

Caitlyn McCarthy

Stuff

What do you think true happiness means?
Just more stuff and gadgets, a gourmet coffee machine
An eight-slice no-crumb toaster, a crispy potato roaster
The pro-steam mach-3 iron for perfect no-starch seams

What would you do without the omelette maker?
The easy clean self-shaking milkshake shaker
The super-eco multipurpose food processor
The quick and easy bakery-fresh fresh bread maker

Where would you be without your curve-edge plasma telly?
The plug-in movement-sensor spray in case the room gets smelly
The artificial-intelligence robotic-drive smart-mower
The multilevel vibro-belt to tone your flabby belly

Could you survive without the max-load tumble dryer
A cordless bagless Hoover and a no-fat deep fat fryer
Would life be dull and empty without a poppin' popcorn popper
A nuclear-powered microwave and atmos-purifier

You clutter up your life with all these meaningless possessions
Inveigled into following the national obsession
To display your wealth and status by the things that you own
Banal, thoughtless consumption with no limit or discretion

Blind, dumb consumerism, an insidious smoke screen
The under-workings in plain view but rarely ever seen
Stuff is not important; it's humanity that counts
Forget about the clutter, forget about 'the dream'.

Christine King

All These Men Around Here - It's Worse Than Tomatoes

Grandma says 'All these men around here - it's worse than tomatoes!'
We laugh - 'Grandma, you're so crazy.'

Grandma says 'Where's my cat?'
We say 'In the conservatory.'
Grandma says 'Where's my cat?'
We say 'She's in the conservatory.'
Grandma says 'Where's my cat?'
We say 'She's in the conservatory.'

Click.

Grandma says 'Why is she in the conservatory?'
We say 'Graham's allergic.'
Grandma says 'Can't we just put Graham in the conservatory?'
We laugh 'Grandma, you're so crazy.'

Grandma gives me a piece of advice 'And remember, if you can't laugh then don't.'
I remember her saying it but I don't remember laughing with her again after that.

Grandma says 'It's time to feed the cat' and puts Heinz Cream of Tomato soup into the cat's bowl.
The cat has been living with Graham and Caroline for the last 6 months but keeping the bowl seems to help.
I clean up the bowl and make another cup of tea and we sit.
I show her a picture of her sister Ellen and ask her who it is.
She says 'Mr Heath'

In the kitchen, my mum and dad clean out the cupboards.
There's a single can of ginger ale in the fridge. It's Canada Dry
except the logo looks twisted and out of date.

There's a jar of pickled cabbage in the cupboard.
It's dated best before 12th of September 1987.
I was born on the 29th of November 1990.
Grandma doesn't eat pickled cabbage.

Grandpap ate pickled cabbage.
He died next door in the dining room.

I always thought that was the catalyst – when it started.
Years later, Mum told me that I was remembering it wrong.
It started before that, when he was still alive.
He knew it was happening and that soon he'd have to leave her
behind.
Somehow that just made it sadder.

Grandma asks me 'Where's my mum?'
Grandma asks my dad David, her son, 'Where's my mum?'
No one says 'Grandma, you're so crazy.'

Grandma asks Keith 'Where's my mum?'
Keith has never met Grandma properly before.
He's seen her a few times when coming home from work or out of
the window.
He's said hello once or twice.
Keith doesn't know where her mum is or why she's standing in his
driveway at 3am.
Keith helps her home and calls David.

Grandma never says David anymore.
She never says Caroline or Susan.
She never says Eden or Bradley or Laura or Rebecca or Madeline
or Jake or Laurie.
She doesn't even say 'Mr Heath'

Every Sunday, I get a text from my dad.
'Hi, do u want to chat tonight?'
This means '*I'm visiting your grandma in the home.*
I've fed her blended roast chicken from the bowl, blowing on it
first to cool it down.
I've fed her juice from the tippy cup and custard.
I've put cream on her face and tickled her toes.
I've brushed her teeth and spoken the numbers 1-10 in French:
Un, Deux, Trois, Quatre, Cinq.
Why did the cat sink?
It's in French because for some reason when she first stopped
being able to talk in English she managed to hold a perfectly good
conversation in French.
That was years ago now though.
I'm texting you because now she's asleep and I'm alone.
I don't want to leave her but she left long ago.'

Whenever I'm home for the weekend I go with my dad to visit.
In the car, he told me once that he feels guilty.
That he should've done more.
That he hates the fact he has to rent her house while she's still
alive to pay for her care.
The house where his dad died.
He makes me promise that if he ever gets like that to send him on
a long holiday to Switzerland.

Whenever I'm home for the weekend I go with my dad to visit my grandma.
She can't laugh, so she doesn't.
But at least sometimes she smiles.

Laurie Eaves

Demolition

'It's been a while,' I said.

Clouds shirked
the cheeks of glass
at such a frequency
I couldn't help but smile.

>   'They left me,' it said.

I stopped,
dropped my jacket
on the garden wall,
my satchel at the roots
of withered daffodils.

'They did,' I said,
pushed the garden gate
grating at the joints.

Swollen from years of storms without a testing hand,
the fat front door chattered on the ridges
of the tricoloured porch.

>   'They dropped me,' it said.

I stepped in, scuffing
the dirt from tiled chevrons
slotted along the passage.

'I know, Darling. I do.'

The living room door
sulked towards the frame.

'It hurts.'

I kicked a Polyfilla tube
across chipboard floor,
plastic clattered into skirting board,
the fireplace spewing scree over the hearth.

'It's not your fault,' I said, 'none of it.'

Ceiling paper sagged
as damp picked the wall paint
into maps - a city without roads.

'Love, it's a lottery.
Someone has to lose
to make it - well... '

Amongst the sofa cushions
piles of wrangled *New Scientists*,
Radio Times, a dozen Dickens Folios
splayed out.

'Help me,' it said

Kitchen cupboards tinned and jarred,
the windows flaking magnolia
while pardoned poppies
leered in.

'Help you how?'

Bike limbs crammed the utility room,
the back door locked,
cat flap gaffered up.
The latch too stiff
to twist from bedded rash.

'Please don't leave again.'

'It was never my choice,' I said.

Upstairs, the ceilings gone,
the roof opened up
to attic beams, rock-wool tufts,
the rooms collapsed into one,
four beds dressed in moss sheets.

I found the bathtub algaed in rust,
a jaundiced toilet bowl,
dirty dolls in the sink.

'Find the heart,' it said.
'Find the heart and cut it out.'

Ivy wreathing taps,
a mound of mothed flannels,
bottles of Matey bubble bath:
pirate, princess, sailor.

'Where?'
It would not answer.

I flung soiled books
from bowing shelves,
sodden letters from drawers,
records from sleeves, from boxes.

Turned bedding over
by the armful,
releasing tattered scraps
from crochet-knots.

Ripped up edges of weathered threads,
unearthed woodlice carcasses,
found

no beating heart, no wooden spoon
or wedding band. No heirloom quilts
or off-white dress.
No empty cots, spoilt nests,
no unvarnished violin.

'Deeper,' it said,
'where the water lags.'

Then I knew.

Took the stairs in leaps of three.
Stains meandering the carpet runners
slinking down each step.

Beneath them, a trap-cellar door.
No light switch. Eyes adjusting
as I neared the puddled ground.

Under the coal grate
in sun beam

a rat

on gathered dust sheets
nursing thumbs of young.

'Do it,' it said.
'Dash their brains out.'

Hilary Watson

The Final Act

Soon after four o'clock, on July 11th 2016
5 uniformed police officers were shot dead by 'sniper fire' in Dallas Texas USA.
Faith in the police, of maintaining order, guardians of justice, upholding their duty, their responsibilities for the safety of all its citizens is challenged, whilst a non-judgmental attitude towards the community as a whole is needed, not easy to predict how the officers shot and, or wounded would have reacted their 'mix of personalities' along with their past experiences, their 'know how' were of no affect no consequence in this instance, nothing would have stopped the victim count rising, not until the sniper was eventually 'taken out'.
'The police were shot dead like dogs, like dogs shot dead
'Bold as brass' can be those who, under fire, swagger, shout, or the few, in panic, unable to reach out for their weapon, their gun
The witnesses, spectators who stand and wait, those who safely stand as from a distance, are the writers from within, to be published in future journalistic stories
'Waiting to be spread'
Waiting ready, able to hold those who blast their firearms, to account
Taking up can take a long time, a long watch with such an incident like this, to gather up
And unravel
A singular or choral activity, an attractive desire to stand centre stage, joy!
A hard mixture in living with the gun, in knowing of it, not using it, doing it, a kind of sinning, at the time forgiving, use of the gun in the important task of saving lives
'And that I guess is how it feels'

Building colleagues territorial placing of chairs with long-term loyalties, in the squad room, stories of bullet damage hitting the target in use, clash and shatter, fracture further, with shells splintering, gorging, piercing beyond skin and face in shattering time,

President Obama spoke of the loss of uniformed dead, sad the divisions within society, of his sorrow, during his tenure of the formidable white and legal gun. 7 officers were wounded on site, during exchange of fire. The political lobby remaining on course, with the black community feeling a sense of injustice, sensing a lack of equality in American culture, steeped as it is in a violent gun history the threat of the gun, gun dog, pit bull menace. Black and gangs with police, now targets.

It is apparent this lack of trust, trust between police and citizens which is ongoing continuous assaults on people within the black community by police, culminating in these violent brutal acts of police killings, picking off the police officers who in the vicinity at the time, paid the price

'And were ambushed'

At the time not seen as happening, then rapidly happening

In a situation where a heavy sense of threat is felt

Where large groups are gathered it's becoming apparent that saving lives with quick and decisive action is paramount

Faith in the police eroding with defiance developing in black populations

Feelings of resentment, a lack of equality, antagonism steeped in American folklaw, the white and legal right to have ownership and use of the gun for sport and protection.

There's pleasure to be had in owning and holding a gun, the attraction of working the gun, holding the gun, power of the gun, in controlling the situation, along with the training required.

Taking out the aggressor is fraught with danger, risks can occur.

Risks deadly and final

17

A battle, in whose hands for the good of others or not, hands or
not
In a world of the ransomed sniper's gun, people fear the fear that
they could be shot, shot again, where they lie, shot dead.

Ronald David Constant

Frozen Socket

These volts no longer connect the synapse,
Shutting down due to overheating relapse.
Over and over, the cooling fan stutters its rotary cycle,
Stoma to coma, frequencies of these voices envelops new rivals.
Cavalier trotting mightily through the valley and the hills,
Until I spill upon my fearing chills collapsing and shattering the
once shimmering chandelier.
This is how it feels to be a frozen socket,
Your emotional locket busted,
Your physical self mistrusted.
Staples pinning you down loosely,
On second-hand paper to which no one helps as you bleed
profusely.
Perhaps that's metaphorical, but the theological methodical
mindset of the mass suits treat mental health like an
afterthought.
What's happened to support,
What catalysed this abhor act: To not olive branch with supportive
rope to give them hope.
But no, we say nope as they gurgle on prosthetic bar soap as they
smoke away their futures I hope you choke
This is not just a poetic verse to divide,
Rather we reside and hide away from love as they're filtered by
the ashtray.
So don't dismay and come out to play. This though is not a game,
So let us all plug and tighten the earth wires to neutral.
So we are all snug in full connection.

Dray Zera

Breasts

Here on my chest are these things called breasts,
I spent many years waiting for them to appear,
sign of womanhood clear to see,
a curvaceous indication of puberty
and attainment of the adult state,
I got them late.

Flea bites, gnat bites, two poached eggs,
it seemed as if the concept had grown legs
and run away to join the media circus,
all the bright lights and fun of a world constructed,
not reality, designed to create inferiority,
to sell, sell, sell, it was just as well
that my own mother was wise to tricks
and dismissed them with the flick of a switch.

I was none the wiser, so I never tried
to hide a body strong and healthy,
I wasn't wealthy enough to afford
a bra in every colour, so it was all white
for me, a symbol of purity,
until my late teens when my wardrobe went black,
I've never looked back.
But how we see breasts puzzles me,
a part of the body subjected to so much attention,
across time a corseted heaving bosom
enough to drive a romantic hero wild,
to the opposite end of the scale where binding
them makes finding them hard a task

for those who wish to mask them,
the flatter the better if you wish you had none.

And what's with the idea that bikinis are okay,
but if you use them to feed a baby, wow, no way!
That's obscene! It shouldn't be seen!
And if you must breastfeed, cover up,
lift your top up, if you pull it down,
people will think you're easy, all over town;
I don't get it, it's what they're made for,
yet society is disgusted and we've mistrusted
our own bodies for far too long - this can't go on.

We use them for pleasure, yet they can be a pain,
with nipple cracks and thrush attacks, blebs and blood,
the stuff of nightmares, but don't worry, relax,
with the right support, they can work again,
be free of pain. And if they can't there are alternatives
and yes, I am glad of those, but I don't suppose
many women know the business norms
behind marketing storms, designed simply
to part us from our money, and the lies and pretence
of added value are really not funny.

As we age, maybe they descend,
our once skyward friends headed south for comfort,
muscle tone changing our shape, our eyes
now focused on other prizes, but don't forget
to check for lumps and bumps and signs
of an unwelcome visitor that could steal away
your life, catch it early, deal it a death blow,
or even take a knife to the very thing you wished for,
removed to save your own life.

We don't talk about older women's breasts,
we look away, as if to say, they are not a thing
of beauty and it's our duty to cover them,
but they don't offend my eyes and we need to know
the spectrum of normal healthy bodies, not shame
and hiding because truths don't match what others
want us to see; truths really make us free.

So give me breasts, boobies, baps or a rack,
bangers, bristols, flotation devices,
threepenny bits, tits if you really must;
mimi, mulks, this side and that,
righty and lefty, this one and that one,
all together and undone, free the nipple
or cover up, do as you please, sitting on the sofa
or swinging from the trees.

Ali Jones

Beauty

No matter how much we deny,
Beautiful people; things; flowers; nature catches our eyes,
Looking at them we get enraptured - forgetting everything,
Eyes give us a feeling of awe, maybe for interim!

Beauty is skin deep, which is true - one layer exposed,
You get gory muscles and blood,
Does it really matter how one looks?
When skin disposed!

When we explore from mind we get hooked longer,
Mechanics of physics, laws of nature, illusion of rainbow,
Intelligence attracts us, one cannot refuse,
But mind doesn't give rest, only amuse!

What really brings peace to soul is the connection with heart,
Do we really care how our parents look?
We just rest our soul and bask in the sunshine of their love,
Connection of heart lasts forever,
No matter how different our beloved/parents look, behave - with time,
Peace, contentment and love - which we feel with them are the signs,

So all that matters is our heart, which is the key,
For all our pure peace and real beauty!

Kadambari Madhok

A Letter To Anxiety

Dear Anxiety,

You make my head spin! You make it so it's hard to breathe and I get light-headed and need to calm myself down. You get me hot under the collar. When you're around I get tongue tied and suffer from sweaty palms (oops, there goes my social life). I gave up caffeine for you and baby I love caffeine but you're the only stimulant I need. My heart races, my mind whirls and I'm lucky to get any sleep when you're around - if you know what I mean. Our relationship is one that makes my friends feel awkward, gains the disapproval of my parents and causes concern for my lecturers who believe because of you I won't reach my full potential.

All of this sounds wonderful but lately I've been thinking. There are some issues in this long-standing relationship of ours. Allow me to elaborate.

Your sporadic appearance in my life makes me question your commitment. You creep in at 3am and grip me so tight that my eyes fling open, heart in mouth, gasping, gasping, gasping at the stranger in my bed, at this unprovoked assault... until I realise it is your familiar presence and knowing it is you, my old friend, makes this reaction so much more acceptable. But should it be?

You force me to remember that embarrassing thing I said days ago, weeks ago, months ago. Muttering in my ear how stupid I am. But darling, I lived through those moments. That 'I hope the world swallows me whole' moment came and went and I am still here. Stop living in the past.

Oh, but you also love the future. You ask the big questions.

What are you doing with your life? Do you think that's a wise career choice? Do you want children? Who will care if you disappear?

And you have the answer to them all. Nothing. Maybe you should waste another five years studying something else, that seems like a smart plan. No you don't, but then what will everyone else think of you. No one.

The longer you stay with me the longer I drink from a poisoned chalice with no signs of coming up for air. Your chokehold causes my face to turn ashen, pinned down whilst your voice makes my bones shake in bruised skin from endless hours of pinching myself because time with you here is not some heady romantic daydream but a living nightmare where things spiral out of control and self-doubt becomes a child nurtured between us that cannot be let go. You have never taken me in a warm loving embrace and quelled my fears only stoked and fed a fire of despair and self-loathing.

But understand this, before you came around I had a voice. Confidence spun into a crown sat upon my head, a queen who conquered life and dared anyone to dethrone her. And in the times when you choose to slope off and visit the girl at the other end of the office, the unsuspecting boy on a night out with his friends or my nan after she has finished her prayers - my voice resurfaces, my lust for life reappears.
This relationship was never one of love and support. Anxiety, you need me more than I need you. Your clingy ways kept me captive but I have bided my time, voice growing stronger, bruises healing and bones reinforced with concrete.

So hear me when I say - it is not me. It is you.

And coffee never tasted so damn good.

Zara Ahmed

The Open Mic

I'd been practising reading the poem out loud all week
and knew each word, each line by heart.
I'd mastered the physical actions,
knew how to get the voice, pacing, articulation and emphasis
right,
knew how to bring the poem to life and captivate an imaginary
audience.
Now, it was showtime.

At nine Greg looked at me and said
we may as well begin
and as I was the only one signed up to read that night,
made my way to the gloomy stage between rows of empty
chairs and empty tables to a place
where a lone microphone haunted a threadbare carpet.

You start, I'll round up a few more people.
Greg disappeared down wooden steps.
I heard a ghostly moan of voices,
the clink of empty bottles,
scraping of chairs and the vague iambic clicking from the pool
table.
So I read to Mark (who sat behind the mixer desk),
the empty room and melancholic dust.

I only reached the end of the first line of my poem
when Mark took off his Sony headphones,
put two fingers across his lips
and disappeared through the emergency exit.
I finished reading the poem's final couplet.

Lights flickered from the room's poltergeist.
There was no applause.

I sat back at my empty table.
Minutes later Mark returned through the emergency exit,
then Greg, the shades of students with skinny jeans,
poets armed with lever arch files, wraiths, devils and vampires
spirited up wooden stairs.
Greg ran onto the stage, took the mic and said
the next reader of the night is...
Steve
who lumbered onto the stage
in his red Che Guevara T-Shirt,
shuffled his poems
and mumbled into the mic
about an old fat guy who had a prostate examination
by a doctor who backed out the door
saying *this isn't going to hurt one bit*
before running back with a lubricated index finger
extended like a lance.

I can't remember what happened
as I'd stopped listening to him
and the others that followed
with their lever arch files, metaphors and bloodied incisors.

I couldn't believe I'd been ignored, disrespected
and was so angry I wanted to climb on stage
tell Greg exactly what I thought of him
and read my poem
but before I could do that
Greg ran onto the threadbare carpet
took the mic and said

thanks for coming everyone
thanks for listening
and see you next month.
Everyone left by the wooden stairs. Greg, Mark, Steve,
students with skinny jeans, poets armed with lever arch files,
wraiths, devils and vampires.

I was left alone with my poem, the one
I'd been practising reading out loud all week
and knew each word, each line by heart.
I'd mastered the physical actions,
knew how to get the voice, pacing, articulation and emphasis
right,
knew how to bring the poem to life and captivate an imaginary
audience.

I looked at my poem again.
They were right
it wasn't very good, so I crumpled it up
and tossed it away hoping that other
better poems
would come along.

Rodney Wood

A Sea Of Choices

I swayed along the sodden shore, a sea of choices at the fore
The ebb and flow, the swell of sea my inner voices prompting me
Encrypted on my ebony soul, fastidious to complete my goal
Husks of shells all asunder, my spirit and psyche's potent plunder
Grains of sand beset the land copious in number
I shall not hasten to perceive in case I make a blunder

Scattered incongruous objects washed up with the tide
An enigma thought-provoking ride
A conundrum compels my mind in fluid verse
A quandary I cradle like a baby's nurse
The cogs of time like the clouds disperse
Spellbound in choices like an ancient curse

Limpets and algae unshackled, sealed to the granite rock
Aloof from my choices, theirs I cannot mock
Deep rock pools of sea water kelp forest waft
Into nooks and crannies of tide gullies aloft
Phases of the moon, tidal current's voice
Precognition concur resigned to Hobson's choice

Eva Appleby

Little Box

I spent all my teens trying to get out of that box they put me in.
It was supportive, I didn't go hungry, never cold.
I guess it was caring,
But dear God it was small.

What's the point of university, we don't go to university.
You want to do art, we don't do art.
Work at the factory with us, find a nice boy, maybe a wee flat by
the time you're twenty.
We'll see wee Jim about getting you a wee works van.

I spent my early twenties trying to fit into my collegiate box.
Life was new streets and virgin blank pages.
A dark box, I was frequently drunk in there sharing eager kisses,
ugly fumbles and cider belches.
Alone in the world with new amours, Joni and Morrisey.

What the fuck do you actually do with an avocado?
A pint of red witch and a lager and lime please.
Yea. I'm on the pill.
No, I don't want to wake up on my own anymore.

Heading to thirty, I was really, really trying to get into someone
else's box.
Hit and miss, miss, miss, dating.
Belly in, lippy on, tits out.
Long dark cornered pauses, punctuated by sips of my Bacardi and
Coke.

Nope I'm really not into dungeons and dragons, no I really don't
want to see your dice.
No, I don't smoke. Yea. I'll dance though.

Yes. I think you're so right, Marillion are musical geniuses and can reach deep inside us all.
Yes sure, I'm free tomorrow, a party, yes I'll meet you in the garden.

At five minutes past midnight on the 16th of August, 1995, I was the bloody box
I got it, I understood the point of it all not just the footnote.
Holding those tiny toes that smelled like digestive biscuits, and me, and soil after rain.
I inhaled and knew the secret I wasn't looking for.

Now how the hell do we do this.
Why can't you watch her while I have a bath.
Yes honey. I will stay with you and doggie till you fall asleep.
And for the last time, there is not a bee in your bed.

Busy with a life I didn't notice when he fell into another box
Her box. Her fucking tidy box, tidy of life and full of a different love.
A moonlit flit and a punch to the heart from two lines of biro stuck to the fridge.
Someone. Close the lid on me and my child, tape us in.

Yes sure I will take her to the park, yes sure you can collect your albums then.
Yes you can keep the coffee maker, yes you can have the toaster.
No I don't have your mother's baby photos of you.
No you can't. Whatever. Yes. Just get out of our lives.

Aged 52 now, too many candle and cake days have passed, and I am suddenly lost in my box.
More of me wobbles than doesn't, more is wrinkled than plump.
I can't get up from a chair now without making a noise.
No more the steady cog of anyone's universe, my perceived omnipotence rusts.

So what now? What happens now? What box apart from the final one will fit me now?
This box is full of memories and smells and sounds of her and me, then and them.
To be alone now in this box crammed full of my life is an odd thing.
Fought for, shared and repaired it is now all I have in my hands, my tatty little box.

My tatty little box...

Audrey Biscotti

My Battle With Eating Disorder

My battle gets harder to fight every day
One of the things I need to survive is the enemy
The ugly truth is love can't save me and
Death doesn't frighten me

The chains that bound me to my obsession are tightening
I'm losing control my desire to be thin is natural to me
Like a mother protecting her child or a lion her cub
Russian roulette the game, skinny the aim

When I look in the mirror I am full of self-disgust
The voice in my head telling me I'm not good enough
Standing on the scale my true weight is revelled
A devastating number and no victory in sight
All I want is to curl up and die than be fat and alive

I am a prisoner stuck in my own body
Becoming a shadow of my former self
No bright light shining from within
A sign that hope has faded away
Looking for a way to set myself free
death becomes me.

Natasha Howorth

Until Morning

Let's stay awake tonight,
I want to stay up all night with you,
Burn the midnight oil and burn our candles at both ends,
And we can greet the enchantment of 3am with heavy eyelids and
lazy grins,
And slay the silence of the hour with words that suit the dark,
And wait to welcome back the sun with reciprocated warmth, the
prodigal sun,
Who left for a while to revel on the other side of the world,
And I can watch as the purple blue rings emerge beneath your
eyes,
Saturn painting an abstract self-portrait on your face,
Let's swing the fridge door open and bask in its lighthouse glow,
Like sailors marooned in a black sea of kitchen,
With worktop cliffs and kettle boats and knife and fork fish that
shimmer silver,
And we can have a picnic on the kitchen floor,
A feast on the seabed,
And unpick each other like strangers, because in the dark you are
unrecognisable,
We can lie on the hallway carpet and let the night fold and wrap
us up like gifts it will give it to the morning,
And I'll count the seconds between each time you blink,
One, two, three,
Let's build a den from fresh linen, a fortress of ironed cotton,
And pretend that hanging bedsheets mark the edges of our
universe,
And you can tell me stories from the collection that overcrowds
your head,
Stories that like a patchwork quilt,

Sew together the fabric of you,
And I'll fill in the blanks that are your missing threads,
And exhaustion, with unabated fury gathered from the day that
slunk into this night,
Will run down the stairs and clamber onto our backs and we will
shrug it off with the ease of cloud nine,
Who shrugs away the stars because he doesn't want to dull their
shine,
Let's sit outside on the patio deckchairs and deafen ourselves with
the muteness of midnight,
Ear drums that burst like balloons under the calmness of it all,
And we'll wait to see the sky be diluted by sunshine cordial,
And we can be white paper people enjoying a watercolour sunrise,
And you can yawn and your chest will rise like high tide,
And those jaws of yours will swallow whole the night,
Gulping back the sleep we didn't quite catch,
And it can hide inside you for a while until you splutter it back out,
And everyone calls it twilight,
We can be the witching hour's mischief-makers plucking the moon
from his high watch,
Dropping him in the kitchen sink water like a celestial bath bomb,
watching him fizz moon dust,
And then you can sit on the landing and I'll call your mobile from
the lounge landline and convince you that all of this makes
enough sense for you to stay awake,
Let dawn praise how tired we are and thank us for giving the night
two companions,
Night gets lonely, so let's befriend him and not our pillows,
And when things start to stir and life around us resumes, we'll
steal away to our beds,
We'll sleep the day long, our night of wonderment still awake in
our heads.

Elizabeth Frances Garnett

Paralysis

2014.
A year like any other
but significant to this girl.
This girl with the whole world
in front of her.
She used to see opportunity,
running at her from every direction,
but struggling to make the connection
between herself
and her career aspiration.

She was choking
on her own mind, her own thoughts
and she knew she just wasn't coping
with the shock of the fall.
It's cool though because everybody is struggling
with something but she's hurting inside
and her mind keeps fighting with the same
nonsensical shit.

Pause though, rewind, take us back in time
to the days when everything was okay
and she could still think straight,
when life was just one big game.
She was only a kid
and the monsters hadn't invaded,
she wasn't frustrated
with the world but it was soon to cave in.

Her mind started spinning like the Mad Hatter's pocket watch.
Staring at the ceiling wanting her mind to switch off
but she couldn't get off
couldn't be strong
and her face was always so long
now.

Fast forward six months -
She began to open up
but she couldn't 'cheer up'
cos her mind was still stuck
and she was dependent,
couldn't stand not being independent.
More crying, less smiling.
More grey, less silver lining.
Entwined in her friends' arms
who could see an end
to all this suffering but she can't.

And now it's 2016,
hardly living the 'teenage dream'
but she's alright,
she tells herself every night.

She sits at home, listening to the drone
of the bees in the cheery summer's air.
She feels out of it and stuck
in her own stupid nightmare.
She's envious of the sun
and how it shines so bright,
leaving imprints on her eyes and she can sympathise
with Icarus.

But it's the night she loves the most.
The silky black glass, with these chips in it
we like to call stars.
The night doesn't bother her,
It keeps to itself.
It follows her as she walks,
this is her safeguard,
her guardian angel,
but she doesn't believe in angels.
Because it's on these nights
that she considers herself,
wonders what part of her gave up
when she began to grow up,
and realised
that everything isn't always alright.

And then the monsters creep in again,
slipping in and out of her thoughts
and she's scared, she's a little girl again
but she's hell's fury and stronger than before.

Sometimes she wonders how she ended up here,
get another round in, drowns her sorrows in beer.
Kisses another and then discovers:
'This isn't who I'm going to be.'

Georgia Louise Stride

Status: Food

Food all ordered, we're at the table,
Chance to talk, now that we're able,
Phone in her hand, 'What are you doing?'
'Connecting Mum!' - An argument's brewing!
I'll join her then, where's my phone?
Chatting with Mum, she's clearly outgrown!
Now I'm on Facebook - what status to post?
A picture of 'good food', not coffee and toast.
Food arrives and it looks so pleasing,
Photo opportunity I'm certainly seizing!
Wait! The angle, colour, effects or not?
Drinks in the picture? The cocktails we got?
Picture taken, I'll post it now,
If I can just remember how
Caption? - I need words too?
This is too stressful a thing to do!
What's the time? Do I call it lunch?
Or is it too early, is it more 'brunch'?
She's finished her meal, I feel old!
Status is posted - but my food's gone cold!

Jessie B Benjamin

Important Questions

Let's ask ourselves important questions
I'll start:
Do crabs think fish fly?
I'm serious.
Do they look up
past the seaweed and go
'Jesus Christ
that is some trippy shit right there'
do you think?

Do you think that we will ever colonise Mars?
But not in the shitty way
that NASA and its 'proper scientists'
with their 'degrees' and
'deep and complex understanding
of the realistic constraints
that go into space travel'
have envisioned.
No.
I'm talking the type in Total Recall
where there are frankly
unnecessarily tall
and fragile glass pyramids
that you, me and Arnie could run around in.

Do you think that they'll ever make a movie about us?
Scratch that,
Who will they cast in the movie about you?
If I had to choose a lead,

I'd say
probably Tom Hardy...
Wh- n- No! No,
not because he reminds me of you,
it's just,
like,
he's got so much range.
The man's a genius!
Alright, I'll try again.

Do you believe in God?
I do,
his name is George Watsky
and Sloppy Seconds reminds me
so much of you
that I wouldn't be surprised
if it was a well-disguised acrostic that spelt out
your name.

Do you like hurricanes?
Me neither,
but the last time one caught me
invaded me, an army
of sheet rain and her name you
saved me.
Without even being there,
I refused to be swept away
because I knew
that I'd see you again someday.

Do you remember what it was like
the first time you fell off a bike?
I do,

I went over a pothole so fast
that I actually left the handlebars
like dropped litter and sailed,
a prepubescent hang glider
into a blackberry bush.
I remember thinking to myself
this will make a great metaphor for love one day
and then I cried for thirteen hours straight.
I wasn't wrong was I?

Do you want to get out of here?
I don't mean the bar,
although the cocktails are overpriced
and the bartender keeps hitting on you
and like: dude. I'm right here.
I mean this city
this county
this country
this arm of the galaxy.
Do you want to visit Orion?
You'd love it there,
there's a bunch of people just like you
lighting up the corners of the void
making each angle a dot-to-dot of art
you'd call them stars
I call them: unimportant next to you.

Do you know you've got me writing poetry,
I know, a bit soppy
but every time doubt or anxiety cracks my confidence like egg
shells
I remember I promised I'd make you an omelette someday.

And I can't cook for shit,
but I've been thinking
if fish can fly,
then so can I so:

Darling,
I've got two tickets to Orion.
I'm gonna go up,
meet Arnie.
So answer me important questions:
Would you like to join me?

Connor MacLeod

The Familiar And The Strange

In this space we call home,
a lusting we don't understand.
Jam tarts, brown paper bags, cruel temptation and undefeated craftsmanship.
If we had a roof, love would raise it.
Smiles beneath rubble, nurture knocks doors off hinges.
We expose our children to the very beams we hide our own eyes from.
Black hats crossing white stripes, floating dogs and flooded streets,
dyspraxia, dis/ease.
Shift patters of black men boxed in,
conveyer belts charge in, fate defying
but never destiny dodging.
Rolling rocks, wise clouds, pipe dreams, silver locket, wise eyes...
Worn window sills where plants grow and love letters transpire...
Complacency is created through love and dedication, that tickles fancies and takes the milk in.
Education is not white
Education is not male
Education is not charged!
I will put my daughter in cute bathers without worry, and let her kick footballs, and bang her head
and wear odd shoes, if she wants to.
Multiculturism, turned from destination, to whitewash operation where money buys your identity...
Outnumbered
Stray dogs - save stray dogs
and it's the turning point that interests me.

Propaganda porn, we act like it's not there, it's everywhere,
in the familiar and the strange.
We hold the heads of our broken men, sat on skulls disguised as quaint pebbles,
while you watch us through glass panes.
Buggies too big for business as usual.
I take comfort in kittens I don't know how to love yet.
Brides choke in the smoke of hope and children visit graves in vain anticipation.
Look. Wait. Read. Hug. Love. Get high!
War is not healthy.
Dress up, strip down, shout, expose, stop!
Synchronise sound systems, viable vigilance.
How shall we escape if we neglect?
Don't spit on me and tell me it's raining!
I'd watch my own father's legacy rot and make mud pies for my enemies
and make them wash it down with warm milk from my dead neighbour's doorstep
while the buoyant bunting blows in the wind.
Toffee apples filled with poison, shadows, spears, beer gardens,
one year guarantees but no part exchange in this cultural extinction.
King-sized mop heads, create the look, pose, gesture, clothing not worthy of focused attention.
Titillating T-bone, veins beyond your years, free-for-all flesh, hair-barely-there clouded perfection.
Broken boy before he's begun,
purple ticket looms in the background,
taunting.
Booze begging, taunting.
Bubbles - the only colour.

Bonnie babies with toy buggies - the only colour.
Be a lover, be a fighter.
Revolution - the only colour.

Rufus Mufasa

Dating In 2016

Little Miss Tinderella
All she wants is a decent fella
6 pictures are all you can see
Plus, a tiny bio 'All About Me'

Just swipe left or swipe right
Or say 'we're going out tonight'
Congratulations you've got a new match
But you never know what you might catch

Bios full of 'the kid's not mine'
Receiving messages like 'Damn you're so fine'
Pictures of stroking tigers a must
Looking in the wrong place for honesty and trust.

Countless married men just looking for fun
Or guys doing the marathon run
Some guys don't even want to impress
They're more interested in getting you out of that dress

It's all great fun while it lasts
Troubled people with baggage and pasts
Not everything is as it seems
Welcome to dating in 2016.

Laura Aimee

Freedom Of Thought

The way the world spins on its axis is accepted and believed,
yet we feel no spinning or turning at any point in our day;
so why do we believe what others say?
Opinions and beliefs affecting us in every way.

There is no purpose to this writing,
it is merely the freeing of thoughts, yet the ego is biting;
'frustrated that I cannot write freely through my own will'
as I begin to formulate a poem with meaning, I lose my feel.

For the words on the page and the depth behind the ink,
my head is cluttered and I am failing to see the link,
self-doubt is what is driving me and that is forever true,
until we rise above these energies and pierce our way through.

The realm of the physical which keeps us grounded and asleep,
wandering around every day circling, knowing not what we seek.
Is it love, money or something of a greater power?
Either way searching for secular entities will leave us feeling sour.

There will be no inner joy nor any fulfilment from the Earth,
but only from within can one find his inner worth,
not from cars, others or even the nicest dwelling,
if we continue down this dangerous path we will consume what
they're selling.

These fancy rings, plastic bodies where nothing is sacrificed,
changing our appearance and yet becoming ever more atomised -
follow the new trends and the latest fashion,
change your faces and your bodies if that's your passion -

But forget not that life is more than what we can physically see,
no outer 'beauty' can set your inner self free -
observation of the society that has been conjured whilst in our
slumber -
keeping us concerned on meaningless things, turning us into
another number.

So how to break free from this hypnotic mechanical feel?
We are becoming the same and forgetting what is real,
let the crowds follow each other deeper into Hell,
the blind, the know-it-alls will speak their minds and tell.

Spreading the word of that which has been falsely crystallised
within,
who care not for their neighbour, but only for themselves always
wanting to win;
this 'light' 'sunny' path we as a society have chosen,
will ruin us, for we see not that we are broken.

The struggle of seeing things that may or may not be,
for who am I to tell you what you can and cannot see?
All I can say is to never accept that which you are told,
test it for yourself and fight on until you are old.

Freeing thoughts from the body and letting them drift away,
my oldest friend although he is gone, showed me the way.
Through the power of speaking my mind I have learnt to let go,
the most important lesson - you will always reap what you sow.

Stelios Antoniou

After I Found The Fear

After I found the fear
I laid there catching shallow breaths,
Waiting for my chest to rest,
And nerves to settle.

They didn't.
I was scared out of my mind into darkness.
Lost in time;

No tense,
No sense-
Intense.

Here I am again.

I frantically seek for light which I will never find.
A fruitless task-
Something like the Holy Grail.
I will surely only ever fail
In my quest for a restful soul.

This timeline in my mind is old.
It auto plays scenes
I cannot seem to delete.
Full colour, HD, 3D memories
In nightmare form.

I try to quickly flick past the horror,
But it is an impossible task.
I can't fast forward.
I've seen this scene a thousand times,

Behind closed eyes
In fear filled sleep;
For the Sandman plans some wicked dreams.
And even though I know this scene
I cannot seem to stop it.
My words drift into cold air.
My voice is vapour.
'Wake up Ace' I say-
But I cannot hear me.
I can only see my frightened freckled face
Reflected in a tarnished looking glass.

That's how it always starts.
It's cold.
It's dark.

And although I try with all my might-

I cannot move.
I cannot cry.
I cannot fight.

As the glass reflects a tiny light,
I stumble on a stalagmite
Piercing upwards to the sky.
A sculptured spear of soulful ice.

I follow a path of endless, jagged, teeth like shards,
Of glass with shattered peaks.
Broken by suspended ice.
Neatly sliced by stalactites
As sharp as knives.

This can't be real,

This can't be right,
This can't be life.

I fall into the starry night.
If I was strong then I could fly,
But I descend into the dark
And wind up on a tree lined path.

The shadows dance to broken hearts.
The echoes roam like reapers.
I'm running now.
I'm stumbling,
It's hard to find my feet;
'Cos I'm scared,
And I'm weak.
And I can hear the shadows speak.
I can hear the shadows creep.
All I can do is weep,
As I reach what seems to be
A rocky beach.

I see an icy lake.
I stand and wait in fear of fate.
I wait for the waters to take me.
I try to walk away but I cannot.
My feet are frozen blocks,

I'm trapped.
I cannot stop the waves.
I look up to the moon and beg
For her to help me.
I fight,
I cry,

I plead,
To be saved.

My tears freeze
As I slowly slip into the blue.
Lost in a lagoon,
Drowning in the deep and
There's nothing I can do-
Except wait for fate to take me.

The only thing left is fear.

I cannot plead,
I cannot fight,
I cannot cry.

I dare not even try.

So I just let it go.
Inhale H20.
My body's filled with light now,
And I will never know
What happened in the darkness-
Or even after light.
I only wake to dream again,
And fear another night.

Esi Yankey

Tilt

We were born
and we grew
watching the other half
hold the world on a stick,
a glazed apple,
they bit into it,
we felt their teeth.

We were told
to trust the system
till it lurched,
an iceberg-struck ship
with life rafts
for only the rich.

We were told
a country
can cut its way to wealth,
watched politicians
walk towards us with knives
hacking away at our lifelines.

We cried in Job Centres,
were steered out
by steel-armed security guards,
were told our crippled limbs
were fit for work,
that our degrees
were cheaper than paper.

Our shoes had holes,
so did our walls,
our rooms were damp,
so were our feet,
we choked on mould,
prayed for old buildings to hold,
were paid fake gold
by corporations
that we handed over to landlords.

We feared the letterbox
it spat out bills,
we feared the doctors
they gave out pills,
we were told to shop,
bored long drops into our credit cards,
deep wells
that we fell into.
We dug our hands into the dirt
for treasure,
found only bones,
remembered
that life sifts away the ones you love.

We danced psychedelic escape routes
into our brains,
greased the palms of dealers,
longed for the world
to shift on its axis,
longed for reality
to tilt.

The world did not shift,
it just grew hotter
while we only felt the chill.
We looked behind the screen,
saw the machinery
of Sky, CNN, BBC,
were told that there was
nothing to see.

We lost hope,
life became a choke rope
tight around our throats.
Then one day
when we were wandering,
shame snapping at our heels,
we caught the eye
of something bigger than us.
Understood then that love had its own mind.
Understood then that love had its own heart.
Understood then that love could speak to us.

A high ringing
pierced through static and chatter,
pierced through all the propaganda,
we saw our shadows
strip off their dark,
stand naked before us
for the first time.
We saw our world
for what it was,
a poison flower
on a frozen stalk,

it snapped.
We shook the frost
from off our hearts,
turned our faces to the sun,
stared into it,
it did not burn.
Our irises
forged strong
from all we'd seen.

The system withered
in the winter
of our indifference,
its candied promises
crushed beneath our feet
as we walked far from it.

Deborah Martin

If Anything, Writing Poetry Has Made Me Even Less Articulate Than I Was Before

Let's get drunk!
On a weekday night!
Very slightly drunker than we really ought to,
So the world goes all shiny at the edges.
Let's listen to poetry,
And pretend we're paying attention
Instead of glancing across the room at each other.
Let's pretend we are listening to music,
Because (I am told)
That would mean we are actually having fun,
And not just over-thinking everything.
Apparently those two terms are not synonymous.
I know, right?
It surprised me when I found out.
Let's pretend we are listening to Beethoven,
Because then we can pretend we are sophisticated and charming.
Some intelligent people
Do in fact genuinely listen to Beethoven,
So if we do,
We might,
Therefore,
Actually *be* intelligent.
Q.E.D.
Intelligent people have good ideas,
And can convince others of their worth.

Let's listen to Beethoven's Sixth Symphony,
Because relatively few people know how that one goes
And they'll be too busy trying to seem
As suave and cultured as we do
To eavesdrop on our conversation.
Let's pretend we are listening to the Second Movement
Of Beethoven's Sixth Symphony,
Because even fewer people will recognise that,
And, of those, a percentage
Won't even be able to explain what a movement even is.
Then I can grin
And hope,
Fervently,
That you don't ask me for a definition.
The really good thing about the Second of the Sixth
Is that although it's sufficiently *Andante Molto Mosso*
To give us a soundtrack to our evening,
It's not overly so,
It won't distract us from our true purpose here;
Between me Googling the music just now,
And by the time I sit down to write this poem
Neither of us will remember what those words even mean.
We'll have done too much by then.
Let's write poems we have no idea how to finish.
Let's think of things we have no idea how to start,
Rehearse them,
And perform them
Underground
Somewhere in East London.
Let's make eye contact
Across a room full of people

Who are still trying to pretend they know what's happening
onstage.
Let's
Make
Eye
Contact
With so many people that no one can be certain
If this poem is about anyone in particular.
Let's hope she realises it's about her.
Let's hope she's brave enough
To do something braver than this about this.
Let's -
Sorry I forgot what I was going to say;
I had the start of a thought
But then lost where I was going with it.
Forget I said anything.

Alexander Woodward

The Air Of Authority

An authority hangs in the air,
Dictating how we should act,
Telling us which rags to wear,
We signed its spectral contract.

It encases us in sensible skin,
Perhaps a *tasteful* tattoo or two
It may permit, if it speak no sin
Or breathe any dreaded taboo.

It weighs down us, the worry
That we may break its laws,
It does so fire us into a flurry
Without any corporeal cause.

Unusual utterances tutted at,
All oddness is overpowered
By those with the thinking hats
The worst kind of coward.

We may still yet break free,
Crush the calm and collected
And voice our own decree
'Go against what is expected'.

Passion is but the only poison
That can fell this cruel beast.
Once engulfed in emotion,
Its hold over us is ceased.

Stuart Peacock

Knowledge Is Power

Knowledge is power
And power to the people is what we preach
But what is power
When knowledge is out of reach
Now the power preaches that education is the key
That a degree will open every locked door
A degree will make your life less stressful
A degree will make your family proud
My dad tells me daily that
If I want to stop being underpaid and undervalued
A degree will be useful
A degree is necessary
So we tell kids to stay in school
To knuckle down and to learn to play the game
Because university is only open to those who can enrol
To those that fit in boxes
To those that make the economy grow
A degree is the key to a better life
But we've forgotten who locked the doors in the first place
As knowledge becomes less and less public
Libraries crumbling under the weight of budget cuts
Textbooks cost half the price of rent
And tuition only rises
So in the absence of paper
Both valued and degreed
I am labelled 'drop out'
In debt to an institution
That neither educated nor accentuated

Government guidelines and carefully selected curriculums
Are deciding the children's futures
As they sit in classroom
discontent and disillusioned
Misinformed and undervalued
Singing we don't need no education
We don't need no stinking teachers
We don't need no books
Because we've forgotten to teach them that education is
accessible outside the classroom
That there's a whole world out there waiting just for them
We encourage them to get the best marks
While forgetting to remind them that their worth isn't found in
ticked boxes and recited answers
Now I'm not saying that schools are bad
Or teachers have no value
But institutions can often limit the mind
And textbooks are biased to a country's perspective
Literature is carefully censored
Music is carefully crafted
As the teachers fight for their right to teach the children
Trying to prove each one's worth
Still they fall through the cracks
Now imagine a girl in a faraway place
She digs among the smokestacks
As leather spines crack
As the fire devours her future
The ring on her finger tightens
Her only chance of escape lay in the bound pages
of banned books
Now imagine a boy walking down a sunburnt highway

Passed remnants of Taliban attacks and American convoys
His book bag is broken and heavy
But he knows
Knowledge is power
And words are weapons in the war on ideas
Books are his teachers
Of love and hate and war
Because yes knowledge is power
And yes education is the key
But the real power is in the
Stories that we share
In the words that we seek
The dreams we dream
And the way we treat each other
All the daily lessons learnt
Not through literal techniques
And lesson plans
So it seems the only real education these days
Is the one we give ourselves.

Nikki Marrone

Hidden Love

I am the night flowers, whose petals,
White in the moonlight,
Sing with colour as the dawn appears.

But mine is the voice you do not hear
That voice inside your head
Which whispers words of love.

I am the scent of all your memories,
Your distant dreams, your hopes and fears
All known to me.

I am the hand which waves goodbye
But never leaves
That healing touch which rests upon your shoulder
Day and night.

I am the air you breathe.
Your sorrows and your joys belong to me
Because your life is mine.

But this you do not know.

For I am the first star in the evening sky
Who with the rising of the moon
Becomes absorbed within the firmament.

I am your hidden love.

Juliet Borland

Good Luck, Teacher!

'Miss, I need to tell sir I've not done my homework,
It's the one about the Battle of Dunkirk,
He's gonna be mad, it's overdue,
But I got confused with who's fighting who!'

'Miss, I've not got my PE kit today,
It's at my Grandma's and they're away.'
'Well, go down to lost property, take your pick.'
'But, Miss, it's time of the month and I feel sick!'

You've got a guest coming in later to discuss contraception,
So listen carefully and have a sensible question.'
'Miss, we just ask Chelsea, she knows innit!'
'Oh my dayzzz, just shut up for a minute!'

'Louise, Mr Sard said yesterday you were off task and drawing?'
'Yeah, cos all that French is reeeaally boring,
When I leave school, I'm just gonna dance,
I'm not even gonna go to France!'

'Where is Chantelle? I know she's here,'
'She's in the toilet, Miss, crying with Leah,
Cos Darren dumped her for that fit one in year ten.
Yeah, the one who used to go out with Ben.'

'Alright, alright and where is Caden?'
'He's bust his lip, Miss, had a fight with Jayden,
It were when we were playing footy yesterday lunch,
Caden kicked him, so J threw a punch!'

'Okay, let's calm down, not cause a stir,
And it's 'was', Joshua, not 'were'.
Brianna, you shouldn't have make-up in school...'
'She always does it, Miss, she thinks she's cool!'

'And what has happened to your tie?
Everything seems to be creeping high?
Roll your skirt down, it's rather obscene,
And take off that lipstick, wipe it clean.

Right, enough of that, a little equation to fix,
What is x when 2x is 6?'
'Miss, you told us yesterday, x is 4.'
'Yes, but that was a different question, we're doing some more!

Adam, please put your phone away,
Or I'll have to keep it 'til the end of the day.'
'You're tight you, Miss, you can't do that,
It's totes brand new, it's proper phat!'

''Fat', Adam, does not make sense,'
'It's with a 'ph', Miss, different tense.'
'Well, that's not a tense issue, that is spelling,
But I'm rather tense and I feel like yelling!

The bell is for me, not for you,
I'll see some of you lesson two,
Take your folders, don't leave them here!
Oh thank f--- it's Friday and nearly time for a beer.'

Jackie Knowles

Unconfirmation

And see in Orlando
There are more of us to be buried,
To be witnessed.
To pass knowingly lost
From temples where silence
Is a new and distant grief
Met with clamouring dial tones
Like prayer for safe passage.

In other places
News anchors use all the wrong words.
Our grammar is still young,
Still sulking in corridors
Pulling pigtails and smoking round the gym.

The curriculum typified us and
Weaponised the words we chose to
Prove that self-definition cuts the tongues that speak it.
This lesson of direction taught us about force,
Showed us public discourse disguised as dialogue
Desperate for some incendiary distraction
Before we found the right words
Buried somewhere between headlines
Where ink baptised us in diagnosis.

We might need to burn down our own language
Until they stop shoving
Semantics down our throats
And mock us for having dirty teeth
Because rather than red tape for gun merchants

We read texts from bathroom stalls.
Willing him to crawl inside radio waves and escape.
Will them to play possum.
Will unwillingly suicide before murder.
Rather *this* conditional right to life
Than changing something named for change.

And the journalists are all talked off sets,
Unwilling to stand when they came for our knees.
Yet we are the ones that remain unheard
When we are the ones that refuse to be present.
Reduced to singular stories, defined again as adults
By panels too busy assuring us we're equal to listen,
Too busy reminding us that love wins
To see how hate is killing people.
Police are killing people.
MPs are killing people.

Our choices could be killing people.

These feelings aren't bulletproof.
They sour in our chests, having learnt
How trauma doesn't give two shits about safe spaces.
How philosophies formed from anecdotes
Disarm echo chambers with academia
Until repeated history is surprisingly unprecedented
And we are much less articulate when we need it most.

Progress is often supposed to be uncomfortable.
Writing change isn't the same as poetry
And I'm scared the words are betraying us.
Turncoat sentences tied to stronger tongues speak for us

When they're able to define us, name us,
Place us in society and obituaries.

So let's unconfirm ourselves and be uncomfortable.
Meet our surmounting silence
With ceaseless, indescribable noise
So that they might pass vindicated, wasteless
And the last ones to be defined for us.

Ciarán Hodgers

Writer's Block

When poetry abandoned me
Words could not be found,
Inspiration washed away with the rain
Because I left it lying around.

Motivation caught a train out of town,
Creativity got on a plane,
My imagination hopped on a bus
And I thought I was going insane!

Left all alone with a useless head
Full of empty meaningless thoughts,
A ballpoint pen hung limp in my hand,
While my brain stretched painfully taut.

Until one night, around 2am
An idea took form in my mind,
I switched on my laptop and started to type
- surprisingly, out flowed a rhyme!

Writing about being unable to write
Felt better than to not write at all,
Perhaps one day I'll have enough writer's blocks
To build a really big wall!

Jodie Walters

Fun

Joy is a tight-rope walker.
One foot wrong and she's over.
She can do the trapeze with the greatest of ease
when it pleases her self-confessed stalker:

(that's me) thirty-three, a cymbal tied to each knee,
and the tears of a clown painted tumbling down;
marching bass on my back beating fake make-up frowns
'til I'm smiling the same way that she does.

I'll be honest though, she's out of my league,
she's too good for me; she's fearless
and footloose and fancy and free.
Funambulists always are, it seems.

Each sequined step taunts me, haunts me,
saunters above my fat clownish feet.
The suspense is enough, not quite edge-of-the-seat,
but still the thrill grips me inexorably.

I last saw her grocery shopping last week,
from behind empty boxes and a spillage on aisle three.
That's when I noticed the same brackish burstings
from eyes lit with rapture when they capture the first thing
that they see. Never me.

Or was it last month I beheld her, waking up from a dream?
Stertorous and sonorous and so full of wonder of
The impossibilities I'd seen; of the hindsight and foresight,
And Aedh's heaven's half lights, of loves lost at no cost

And the beauty between?

No. Was it last year, could it be, when last she saw me?
Full of sighs I had been, with no hope of reprieve: custard lies
Sweetly whispered left me half-blind and a little unhinged.
It's funny how time can distort all the joy that Joy brings.

She hides from me still, in the edge of a moment,
behind the most mundane things. But recently I've found her
given to making strangers, strangely taking joy in dangers,
walk the rope-thin road to ruin beneath the main marquee.

Happiness is happenstance. Sometimes sweet, but also sour.
No balance in what time is worth with what's paid for every hour.
There's joy above and joy below, and a joy in every step.
A joy that only you can know, a joy you might regret.

Still they're hell-bent on elation. A feeling or sensation
just to justify their lives as they think their lives should be.
As for me? I'm content for once to sit here, a little red-nosed yes,
but who knows what sky-high joy around the corner we might see.

Dan Hartigan

Arbitrary Forces (Put It On The List)

The yin and yang are having an equilibrium moment
The positive is developing a negative attitude
Buddha is not amused
(Black, white and green)
Zen is never mean
Though immortal Zeus can be obscene
Unnoticed, Icarus is still falling from the scene
'Stunning' shouts the clown 'it's all so serene'.
The Buddha is happy to be a little zen, zen
Zoroaster is caught between good and evil
Then and now, now and then
While the Zend-Avesta
Mixes with the Chinese 'peach'
Prompting immortality to reach
The next level.
While below the 'shadow biosphere'
Is proof life has existed
On multiple occasions.
The chimera is blazing
With wild and unrealistic dreams
Its serpent tail is writhing
A nightmare, drowning in Greek myth.
Deep volcanoes explode beneath,
In the dark oceans, as foretold
Where weird creatures dissolve
Like Higgs boson
Invisible to behold
An unlikely home for hairy snails

And sea cucumbers who converse with black smokers
A second coming is imminent
Quick ban all the criminals, fools and jokers.
'We are all beneath the blossoming rose'
Shouts Apollinaire, 'Where the rose gods dance nakedly'
But he knew Picasso you know
The sixth note C major is Atomic (you know).
So, luminous bodies ascend in Auric Eggs
And away we go. Ha, ha, ha, ho-ho-ho
As others stagger towards the twelve basic
Building blocks of fundamental life
Particles governed by four forces above and below
Which can drift and float in parallel universes -
The Vikings are fighting
In their dragonships
While I create this arbitrary 'list'
The Auric Aura closes around the universal dust
The building blocks of matter
Suddenly burst and bust
Meeting with electrons
In a field of atoms, there is love.
We are all massless
Pure light, like Jesus Christ.
Lovers, Romeo and Juliet
Aimlessly decide about life
Eventually making the wrong suicidal choice
About the exit approach
Of which there are three:
1. Time travel - stationary speed.
2. Astral - Gliding through the Energy Fields.
3. Pure energy, smash the protons - Heaven, that's for me

A powerful positive lift, a sacred gift
Stop the 'list'
It's time to get off, time to go
An option I cannot resist.

Graham Peter Metson

Breathing In The Blue

Azure, cyan, powder, cerulean
The sky is a silk scarf over my eyes
Faint scents of cinnabar,
Lavender, roses
Soft folds feel weightless and cool on my hot skin
Hints of herbs where it touches my lips
Breathing to a slow count,
Visualising.
Cobalt horizon joins perfect navy where the fish leap in memory
From Prussian-tipped waves.
Eyes closed in darkness sensing the noon sun, face tilted to
sapphire over the park.

I open a channel to a place where the words had stuck
Where illness had hidden
Where the tears still pool

Indigo, iris, royal, viridian
Almost in touch with a distant vibration, a fluttering spirit, a small
thing awakening.
Blue like her jewels which I find myself wearing,
Blue like cornflowers and his eyes and mine,
Blue like the song which plays in my head now
Breathing in the blue

Tonia Sorrell

Dragons

He believes in dragons.
They're currently his favourite animal.
Last month, it was tigers.
Three days ago, I marked his science test paper.
Question five: Name four living things.
His answers:
1. Dog
2. Cat
3. Tree
4. Dragon

The red ink stained my palms like blood
the moment my pen hit the paper.
I had become Lady Macbeth
and all the perfumes of Arabia
could not sweeten my little hand.
I'm employed to facilitate the broadening of young minds.
How dare I tell this eight-year-old boy
that dragons don't exist?

Now we're in the classroom.
I hand back every test paper apart from his
and tell him I want to see him after class.
His nostrils begin to flare
and I know that if I gave him back his paper now
he'd screw it up into a ball
and use it as kindling to further fuel his fire.

After convincing him that he's not in trouble
(and bribing him with stickers)

I finally get him to agree to stay behind at the end of the lesson
but he still insists on lining up with the other kids
before pulling up a chair next to my desk.

I get out his science test paper.
I refer to question five,
complete with my scribbled out annotations.
I point out the glaring error.
'I'm sorry' I say.
'I made a mistake.
We all make mistakes sometimes, even teachers.'
'That's OK, Miss. I think you're a good teacher' he says.
'Thanks' I say.

'Hey, Miss?
Didn't you say your dad comes from Wales?'
'Yes, that's right.'
'Oh, I love Wales. I've never been there
but I've heard it's beautiful.
There are mountains and valleys
and lots and lots of dragons!
Hey, Miss?
Have you ever seen a dragon?'

I see the longing for magic in his eyes.
I take a deep breath.
'Yes,' I say
'I've seen a dragon
and it was magnificent.
But do you know what?
Not everyone can see them.
I guess I must be really special, like you.'

He smiles, contented with my answer.
I'm teaching him maths, English, and science.
He's teaching me to believe in dragons again.

Carys Hannah

A Memory

I remember the day, you sailed away
It's locked inside my heart
I never thought you would leave me
I did not think we would part

But a far-off land, beckoned you
Your dreams you wanted to pursue
So much to gain, a whole new life
But leave behind a new wed wife

I remember what you told me
This chance you had to take
Our life would be transformed, you said
Our future this would make

I knew you would return to me
All your letters, told me so
I prayed that you still loved me
As it was your choice, to go.

But you see my heart, still bears the scar
Although it's long ago
For I was young and so in love
More than you, will ever know.

Angela Soper-Dyer

I Love Ikea

Ikea Ikea

I
Know
Every
Aisle

Ikea Ikea
Your resistance is futile

Ikea Ikea
You think you've got style?

When it's got its own pile at your local tip
And you don't know if you've got wood or recycled plastic

I sheepishly shuffle with my hangover hard-on
Which like a Krokig clothes stand you could hang a hat and coat on
But this is in no way a reflection on the walnut erection of a beautiful bookcase called... Billy
Behind which I scuttle to disguise my docile protruding (willy) complementary pencil

Ikea Ikea
It's what the weekend was made for

Ikea Ikea
Spend a day with your in-laws

Ikea Ikea
Euro sceptic are you sure?

That your faux leather footstool is derived from old norse
That your favourite meatballs might be derived from horse
Of course you're a big fat hypocrite... but don't let that put you off
As there's nothing more English than standing in a queue
Blaming the size of the small Daim bars upon the EU

Ikea Ikea
Chill out and relax

Ikea Ikea
Why not check out the Gravadlax?

Ikea Ikea
Choose a wardrobe called PAX

And then swerve your way down to aisle 23
Past flat pack families in mid-scouse mahogany
Oh those love handles and eyelashes they don't - come - free
I'd say it's too Konstig but it's Swedish to me
To take a trip to Ikea to concuss life's monotony
To take cardboard cake and refillable coffee

ABBA please!
Take a chance
Take a chance
Take a chance on me
Is this why you chose divorce over double monogamy?

Ikea Ikea
It's a slow and painful death

Ikea Ikea
Buying coffins made of MDF

Ikea Ikea
Take a sharp intake of... breath

When you realise that the bastard won't fit in your car
Cos you don't own a Volvo but a Vauxhall Corsa
Your wife might divorce yer there's nowhere to hide
Why not build the fuckin' thing and just... climb inside

You don't own a hearse so there's not much you can do
Stuck between the blue devil and the... M62

Stephen Quinlan

Besotted

To you beloved love would lead me once in secrecy.
Now it guides me to your side.
So will you follow me to a magical place I know.
A special garden unknown to anyone else
It's a secret nest where roses are forever in bloom
And their heady perfumes lift the soul.
And at night nightingales fill the air with their songs of love.
Only if you come with me will my heart stop its yearning
And I will take you to that nest of dreams
There we will lay on a cushion of soft downy feathers
And your mouth I will shower with gentle kisses.
While your heart so warm and tender will fill
With iridescent dreams.
Let us embrace this magic and lay together lovers
In an enchanted bliss.

Tony Beeby

Cats Leave Home

It should not have ended like this
this undignified mess
I should have gone with her.

She clattered upon the garden fences, absorbed the startled
shapes and froze
her eyes of cyan blue that fixed us and white fur matted on
sickened gut
bolder now within her years an inborn reflex honed to act
she bowed to tense her waning quarters and sprang the fours
upon the grass
towards on weary undulations crept and hung her heavy head
with distance kept a rise to upright and curling tail around to neat
without a choice she sat surrendered, still and patient, withheld
and weak
you held the food she held position and slowly fed when you
withdrew
the outhouse door was pushed to open she raised her chin and
turned and knew

she stayed and shared us that bright summer did we now own
her? Is she owned?
we told the story, our little lodger until the morning of
autumn dew
then we saw her moving slowly limping from the outhouse door
limping, hunched and slit determined towards the hazels and
her death
between the twisting of the garden from the shade she turned
to look
a push of spit and rhythmic licking she bit the weakest limb awake

she brought in air and present senses the steel of now
herself regained
she coiled and leapt beyond the fences and shocked, she gasped
and veered and ran
and left us here with weary autumn, our lion of spring time, our
summer last

cancer bleaches the best and tenses a hollowed weak and
whitened mask
describes this sunken face a wasteland with jutted sharp and
bony edge
the tensing pale and shiny skin that veils a ropey twitchy vein
the strangest scene when you recall our youth, our pride, our
holding tight
should I bare each loving half smile that fronts your shocked
exhausted eyes
whereby their guilty speckled pall will choose this time to look
and lie
I should have gone to the shaded corner the sheltered refuge cool
and dry
with silhouettes of barks and grasses that merge to bring a god
or void
to see the last through sparkling sun and breathe the final sigh
or purr.

It should not have ended like this
this undignified mess
I should have gone with her.

David Fitzgerald

Grandad's Mirror

The light guides me home
Its ray of magical light shines directly in my glistening eyes
I can hear the music which unfolds mysteriously through the
Gold of the old sacred mirror
My grandad's mirror he gave it to me before he died
He said to me it will help me get through dark days
And give me life in the new days.
When I need life most it will come to me
The mirror speaks to me, tells me that a guardian is watching over
me
And that the doves can be released through the magical skies so
they can be
Replaced with life.
My grandad's mirror truly holds powers inside his magical palace
The place of his home, his garden I place it in his green house
And let the sun take form of its magic I then give light to its grace
and pray to God
God replies your grandad's mirror is working
It is giving you more strength each day
It's giving you hope and consolation
You may think that you have darker days since your grandad
passed but look to the mirror
See his crystallised face through the eye of the beholder
Look forward, look on
See him and pray always
Talk to the mirror like you talked to him
And then all you ever wanted will become
Reality.
Okay God I will

I look to the mirror in the stained perfected green house
And see the magic
The magic that was born in this mirror
As I am transported into the mirror
I am a new person I am free
Not alone and not on my own
Anymore, I see my grandad for the last time he talks to me
Then destroys the mirror
You don't need this anymore
The magic is already within
It's within your heart.
And soul
Look for it my dear granddaughter it has always been there.
I smile at my grandad and we both touch my heart
I am transported back to life with no mirror; it could not have
been a dream
It must have been real
And that moment was real
The mirror had been destroyed
I had spoken to my grandad
And now I am well, living life just like he wanted me too
Not thanks to the mirror
But thanks to him and my heart.

Leanne Drain

Walls Pt3

We build walls, we build walls,
We build walls so high.
That they nearly reach the sky,
When all we really need to do is reach out.

We hide our feelings,
Never show ourselves compassion.
Stop opening up,
Never communicating our passions.

We have stopped interacting,
With our fellow man.
Never look in anyone's face,
As we are rushing past.

We build walls,
We build walls so tall.
That they nearly reach the sky,
When all we really need to do is reach out.

We never express,
Our darkest emotions.
Sleeping with anger,
In Ikea beds.

We buy throwaway items,
At extortionate prices.
To store them in cupboards,
Till we donate them to charity.

And we build walls,
We build walls so high.
That they nearly reach the sky,
When all we really need to do is break out.

Break them down, break them down,
Little brick by little brick.
Until the wall is nothing,
Until you believe that you are something.

We never believe,
That we can fly.
Like beautiful kestrels
Soaring up to the sky.

We drown in guilt,
And self-denial.
Punishing ourselves,
With alcohol and needles.

Break them down, break them down
Little piece by little piece,
Until that wall is nothing
Until you believe, you are no longer inconsequential.

We never believe,
That we are worth it.
Compare ourselves,
To the folk in the papers.

We never believe,
In our innate capability.
To survive and bounce back,
From our own twisted journeys.

We don't believe that we are heroes,
Heroes to many.
To the children who love us,
The wives that we marry.

No; instead we build walls, we build walls,
We build walls so tall.
That they nearly reach the sky,
When all we really need to do is break them down.

Matt Humphries

Growing Up

A colouring book becomes Facebook.
Twitter isn't just the sound from a bird.
Mobile devices hold us hostage
to high definition
when ambitions are blurred.
Light-up trainers become stilettos
that shush insecurities
and tightly crush toes,
flashing in the strobe lights
of newly found adventure.
Twinkle twinkle little star.
Nursery rhymes become
bass guitars
that shatter parents' patience
with every beat,
every unmade sheet,
every stumble home late,
every bittersweet
sight of growing wings.
But we carry childhood with us,
a valuable antique,
the teddy bear that hoards dust
at the back of our shelves.
And our days are a game of hide-and-seek,
coming ready
or not
to find ourselves.

Eva Curless

Comfort

Comfort;
1. A state of physical ease and freedom from pain or constraint

Your lungs collapse weekly and your mind doesn't let you think -
there's a pain on your skin and blood mixes with the water flow.
You're bleeding through your fingers when you're sure no one can
see, emotions short circuiting in mind and you can feel them
jumping ship.
You're burning from the inside out, you are smoke and fire
reversed.
It's killing you.

2. The easing or alleviation of a person's feelings of grief or
distress

You're sat for hours and lights don't look the same.
You press a blade into the flesh of your legs, arms, hips, ribs.
Your hair is red again, hides the thoughts leaking into your
hairline.
Matches the lines carved into your skin.
When did you become the thing you were running from?
You're too scared now to scream for help, can see it in their face
they're losing you and hope.

3. A warm quilt

Your body won't move and for the longest time your sleeves are
suffocating and you're hot.
With eyes, red-rimmed, you're passed out in the early hours of the
morning and the sun no longer is enough.
You sink your teeth into the skin of your lips. Speaking blood, you
can see, the reflection, with the broken smile.

A bitter vessel of darkness and anger, a hostage of your own mind.

4. A verb

Marked for selfishness when I sleep because my body feels as though it's giving up on me when my mind is a constant stream of 'they hate me' and 'do something'.
There's blood seeping from the cracks and I don't think they notice as I scrub blood from the carpet and once I took apart a razor, looked over my bleeding fingers, and told them I was bored and they cried with the room.
It feels like an illness and I used to cry every time but now I don't think the hands are my own until after.

Kiera Rees

The Masterplan

Clean cut.
The cut is clean, and yet, still pushing, pushing -
Bubbling and fizzling and jumping under
The surface of my smooth skin,
Are electrodes.

And I don't know
How could I know
Because I never learned such things,
Because why would I want to-need to-ever know
How to stop a Bomb -
How to cut the right cords ?
Before the whole damn system
Explodes
In a shower of electrodes,
And lymph nodes.

And I am almost naked, and something tells me
That in this whole world
We are all naked underneath our clothes.
All built with electrodes, and Zinc anodes.
From the fig leaves Adam chose
To high fashion robes
We are still covered in skin below,
A mannequin automon
Whatever clothes we put on.

All of us are living with a time bomb -
Someone just has to switch it on.
Before you know it, you'll be gone.
Blown to pieces, God's kingdom come.

And who will clear away the doll like,
Ever quavering, quivering, shivering
Once living parts, appendages,
And build us up again -
So we may be explosion free -
Not mice, but men.
What will God do then?

We plague this Earth
A hundred billion dark shadows,
All of us still bone and marrow,
Crawling too closely, shadowed -
Like Peter Pan.

Life's too compacted now,
Wait for the big bang...
Once it goes off, that's the
Masterplan.
The Clockwork Orange is the key part
For this bomb is each and every human heart.

Where will all the parts go?
We are mechanically organic,
And as God made man in his image
We will be rebuilt, but
Our electrodes showing.
The Clockwork Orange glowing.

And yet, it is in the not-knowing
That we are just cleverly-made machines
That keeps us clinging to our dreams.

Inside my body are silent screams.
I did not expect to find this.
I do not know what this thing called life -
This fragile, and yet persistent sequence of systems
Truly means.

Unless what we call dreams are life
And what we call our life, are dreams.

Margaret Sayers

The Sum Of Everything

Fate is my foe, time my enemy. My life pre-designed.
I'm standing on the edge of my forever
On a path, with no map and no navigation.
I smile at my past, my evolution.
From broken hearts, bad relationships, scars and tears,
To a strength, resilience and determination that will carry me
through my years.
I stand tall in the mirror of today, proud of all I have achieved.
No matter where I have come from and what I have done,
No two experiences will ever be the same.
I step forward on my path in the present
Ready for battle and celebration
Knowing that today is the start of my destiny
That tomorrow a new day begins.

Gemma Perrott

Confession

His lips: blood-orange red.
His eyes: a teenage-crush shade of hazel.
Me: a fumble of words unsent.

I've known you too long to fall for you now.
I tell myself to stop waiting,
staring at screens as if they are
portals to your heart
but it's all I do.
I want you to take my hand
and for the gesture to go viral,
to brush along the warmth of my cheek as I blush,
trace down to my chin
and lift my mouth to meet yours.
I can feel it, the gentle bow of your head,
me greedily catching your kiss, ripe
and syrupy with rain, your lips a gift
you will never know I am longing
to hold between my teeth.

I think of sending him this as a Facebook message
but can already predict the 'Seen 21:09'
and the embarrassment of not receiving a reply.
It's probably a touch on the intense side
for a sober Monday evening.
But poets are intense
and that's about the only excuse I have.
For any of this.

For loving you the only way I am brave enough,
through the secret language of words addressed to no one,
the letters of your name left scattered on the keyboard.
You, a treat of overgrown-stubble
flecked across smooth-line jaw,
could be anyone.

If I were to hide clues like:
bus stop - drunk on red wine,
Queens Wood - tea on leather sofa,
grass between fingers - the swell of jazz on a Sunday afternoon,
then perhaps he might know,
but be neither sure nor brave enough to ask
because he is poet, like me
and we both vowed to never date 'one of us'
because it ends in messier versions of *this*.

My lips: a dry, pale shade of blood-red.
My eyes: green with wanting to be your not-so-teenage crush.
You: a message saved in drafts.

I've known you too long to fall for you now.

Georgina Jeronymides-Norie

Love Letter From A Mobile Phone

You've been watching me for hours now,
Pretending not to.
Perched just far away enough to seem
Indifferent, but that doesn't stop you
From casting furtive glances at me
Every thirty clock-ticks,
And the attraction - from my side, at least -
Is electric.

The day we met, you said that I was perfect:
Just what you wanted.
The perfect shape: slim, petite, but with curves
In all the right places.
You said you hadn't seen many faces
Like mine.

And I thought we might
Have lived in each other's pockets;
Found a balance in taking and giving,
And learned to listen
To the things we didn't say.
But communication was never your forte.
I'm not sure it's mine, either.
And though I'd give you anything
You were never much of a receiver.
So, perhaps it's just as well
That our silence is awkward;
That you never ask for more;

And that when it comes to pockets, well,
I only live in yours.

But I'm hung up on you.
And even though, as you reach
for my body, I know
It isn't my voice you're craving,
It's okay.
Your hands found me first.
And as you cradle me closely,
Palms clammy and cold,
I don't care.
I fit so perfectly there.
It's as if I was made for you.

So hold me. Pull me closer.
Brush your lips against my ear.
I will hear whatever you have to say.
I know it isn't meant for me.

But as you speak, I'll press my face
To yours, and strain to kiss
The corners of your mouth.
Falling short, I'll settle
For your cheek

Because I know
That you'll misread all my signals;
I'll never be a long-term thing -
Two years, at most -
And the only ring

In our relationship will be mine:
A shrill reminder
Of all your other options.

Sarah Parker

Jericho

The outer castle walls are ancient stone and strong
My defences built up, resilient,
Unchanging over time,
I stand firm, steadfast,
Confident in my knowledge,
My power, the strict teacher.

Except...

On the inside I am
desperately
Trying to keep it all
From tumbling down,
Running to reinforce the barricades
Covering the cracks.

I cannot let them know.

For I am Jericho.
And I await the trumpet sound
I know and dread will come
And the walls come tumbling down.

Glynnis Morgan

Envisioned

The conscientious monarch completes his duty.
Banishing the enemy *loathed* to achieve his aim,
He plunders this small dynasty, now his own empire!
He becomes the core's sovereign,
Only to dominate as a sanguinary tyrant.

The territory, constructed and amassed by the only ruler,
Capitulated, with all defences diminished.
The King bows his head back,
And bellows a bone-chilling growl.
What has he accomplished?

The sunstone now avoids the moonstone:
No longer needing its dark luminescence,
No longer craving its comforting abilities.
Repudiated, no longer being accepted, the latter -
Enclosed within a box where no soul can recover the abandoned.

The sunstone, observant and raw,
Exposes its focal virtue only to display
The true rotten essence of its creation.
It no longer requires the moonstone!
But what has it accomplished?

Agents, back to back, mounted -
Through thick and thin, they safeguard.
They strive in the deification of their project;
They pursue onwards, battling, in their path.

Will these petty impediments prevent them?
'*No!*' Both agents roar with all ardour,
Vehement with all perdurance.
Protecting their souls: co-ordination!
But what have they accomplished?

Immolating all that he possessed,
For the love of his life...

Ceding all that she contained,
For her tailor-made counterpart...

Endeavouring, but to no avail.
What has this pair accomplished?

Mantaaqa Asif

Application

Upon completion of this job application
Please forward direct to our administration
Along with three copies of your certification
As proof to the management of your qualification

When we have read said application
We may possibly issue an invitation
With a time and a date for interviewation
And in all probability - humiliation

We question you on your education
Your hobbies, background and orientation
To add fuel to the fire of our investigation
We will also require a presentation
We will then decide if said presentation
Makes you worthy of our organisation

If appointed we demand dedication
Loyalty, long hours and appreciation
In return you'll receive remuneration
Which will not be open for negotiation.

Thank you for attending your interviewation
At the appointed time in the correct location
We have considered the ideas in your presentation
And will use them to develop our organisation
However, we're unable to offer you employation
As the boss' son has returned from vacation
And due to the in-house collaboration
We have no need of your expertation.

From: Mr Bare-faced Cheek and his Arsehole Son.

To: Mr Bare-faced Cheek and his Arsehole Son.

Thank you for your communication
Regarding the matter of my failed application
I'm pleased to report I've gained employoation
With the government Office of Business Taxation.

Now it seems I'm under an obligation
To advise you of our investigation
For it's clear your figures are pure fabrication
And you've fiddled your books for tax evasion

Can you guess where you'll be sending your next vacation?

From Miss One Step Ahead of You - Rebecca Robinson.

Catherine Scott

I Think Too Much

I think too much

I'm always doing it

While others sleep
Round the place I do creep
Trying to find ways
To empty out the strays
Those thoughts that run through my head

I think too much

About everything!

Should I have said it?
Should I say more?
Do I go back and open another door or... stay away?

I think too much

Instead of doing what others do
Saying what is true
No matter what others think
But this takes me to the brink of of of...
Thinking too much

Even when I close my eyes
I realise then, this makes no reprise
It's it's it's it's
like the crawling of the flies
Their desperate tries and tries
To escape, to get to the outside

Just to survive
But in my mind's eye
It's all just tall lies
'cause 'cause...

I think too much

There... I'm doing it again!
And just when I think that I have stopped
it's started again

I think that's why I write
Because of or in spite
And it comes out in a rush
Or sometimes at a push

Maybe I'll pen a line or two then I can stop

But that's not the truth
As like falling from the roof
With your safety harness aloof; you'll do it again

Why won't it stop?
Why can't I stop?

Others tell me to,
'But it's easy for me, why not for you?'

I think I will explode: *Pop!*
Take me to the docs, I cannot stop
He'll give me a drop
Or a pill I can pop

But that's not the way he comes out'n says
'It's all in your head'

'You must think about it instead'

But but but doc; that's the bloody problem

I think too much!

Duncan Jay

Weapons Of Peace

The pen;
Mightier
Than the sword.
Words inspiring peace and love
Amongst
The most powerful weapons of all.

The paintbrush;
A power tool.
If used correct,
To the truth,
Its workings,
The people, it can connect.

The guitar, bass and drum;
More potent than
Any
Bomb.
Even
The atomic one.

For you can
Heal the world
With just one
Poem,
Painting,
Or song.

Simon Chambers

In Canada They Call It Tylenol

They took you to the hospital,
vodka-split and pill-riddled –
did you know that paracetamol
are called tylenol in Canada?

I wouldn't have known
if it wasn't for you.

You spoke in tongues to the paramedics,
regressing to your five-year-old self
who couldn't understand the other wains
with the familiar accent and unfamiliar words.

Your parents gave in and taught you English
because your ma said nobody knew how sweet you were;
because you kept coming in from the street
crying and your da thought if they were bullying you,
he ought to know.

I don't know if you cried in the ambulance,
I don't know what Irish for 'help me' is,
I don't know if you asked for help at all
or asked them to let you go.

I shook your parents' hands at the hospital
because it's a luxury that we don't have to know
if you were sorry that you tried –
they would've known
what you were trying to say.
You say you don't remember
but I do –

I wasn't there but I know,
that in Canada
paracetamol are tylenol
and you're not supposed to
exceed the stated dose

(two every four hours,
no more than eight in twenty-four hours)

or wash them down with cinnamon-flavoured vodka –
you've been a whiskey man ever since I can remember,
even since I learned that there's little difference between
dearthair céile and dearthair.

I don't know what paracetamol are called
in Irish, and I don't know
what you wanted your last words to be.

I know that French and Spanish didn't turn out to be
the most useful languages to take in school,
I know that Irish is a dying language and I wish to God
I knew more.

Keshia Starrett

Keep Hanging On!

I'm hanging on by a thread. I just want to let go.
Life will be easier for those around me I know.
I pull them down, I can't wait for them to see me,
The beautiful life and the person I should be.

The forever world, we are hoping for, is just around the corner.
Just keep holding on for just a little longer.
Hanging on tight finger ripped from the rope,
but I can't let go, and lose this hope.

The illness is crumbling my body away,
sinking into the shadow of darkness and dismay.
Just a fingertip left I'm going to fall.
I can't hang on any longer. It's time to give up it all.
I take a deep breath and let go and pray.
Please look after my family and tell them I love them some way.
I'm falling I cannot stop.
It's too late now, falling into the deep drop.

But then something grabs me and pulls me back.
Pulling and pulling me screaming at me don't let me down. You're
stronger than this they gave me the look, the frown.
The anger in their eyes, why don't you lean on me.
I'm here to carry you to set you free.
I can't take away the pain of life that you have to live.
But a shoulder to cry on and tissues I can give.
You're not alone just tell me what I need to do.
Rely on me I'll help you through.

The good, bad and ugly days who cares about those.
Look to the future and the brightness it shows.

Do not fear the loose thread in the rope, and never let go.
Because no matter what happens, this you must always know.

You will always have the courage to hold on tight
we're in this together to finish the fight.
So keep holding on no matter how much rope has gone,
and remember even by that inch of thread you can live on.

Rebecca Hughes

Kiss My Killer Karma

Is your killer conscience breathing?

Justice screams river scarlet blood,
My dark-velvet spirit roars,
'Cough up jet-black karma!'
'Vengeance!'
Tumbles, twists and soars.

Will my soul seek the recipe of revenge?

I've cooked a treacle tart,
Lemon golden and honey bittersweet,
A syrup slap and scrumptious soaring smack,
Killer karma tastes a treacle treat!

Can you feel the dark force rising?

Like a stab in the back,
Killer karma pays the price,
What goes around bites back around,
Chews you once or even twice!

When will you face the curse of karma?

Killer karma strikes behind,
Swiftly swings before your eyes,
Actions always catch us,
You can run a million miles!

Is the spirit of my soul suffocating?

My silhouette soul gushes poison,
Like a river runs and dies,

Scars twirl as dark death rises,
Kiss goodbye to eternal suicide!

Will you live to regret the aftertaste of black karma?

My buttermilk soul sleeps softly,
(Think twice before you harm her)
Don't say I didn't warn you,
When I come for you...
Prepare to kiss my killer karma.

Is your killer conscience breathing?

The taste of your jet-black medicine,
Are you enjoying your jet-black taste?
Drink up, serve up, stir up,
Cough up karma in your face!

Will my soul seek the recipe of revenge?

Justice screams river scarlet blood,
Bloodshed wounds awake; uproar,
'You will pay for bloody murder,'
My light sunset spirit soars...

Drink up, buttercup, drink up, taste your bittersweet and sour
syrup!

Nabilah Afzal

In Marriage

Do your part
Build my self-esteem
Support me in marriage
Do not laugh at my dreams
Remind me to love deeper, in marriage
Do not touch me so deep
When my word, stop, is taken seriously
Do not disguise wrong
Conclude you and me as good
I am not a playing field for a game of thrones
You can rule as King in my woods
But give me a place in royalty too
Show me what loyalty can do.
Apologise with your eyes and not just your words
I will respect the effort as much as this hurts
I know depression, in marriage
I know regret
I saw my mother
I know what is next
Do not leave these memories lying around the house
Leave me exposed lying on the couch
Do not leave these pictures hanging on my walls
Leave me to explain the resistance marks painted from your paws
Simply do not touch me
Emotionally, physically, I mean literally
Do not touch me
If your intent is to empty me
Do not fill me with lies

Teach me to identify true love, in marriage
Allow me to identify true touch, in marriage
Train me to stand for my rights
Not to let people taint what is mine
My 'stop' should always mean stop
You should have taught me to feel like more
Not second guessing your smile as I walk through the door
It was your job to teach me to identify trust
But you have not taught me that much
Father, I cannot see a future with a man who loves me
Because 'love' has taken its toll
Father, your fingers comb my thoughts
And leave tangles in my skull
Father, you were not supposed to make me scared to let men stay
All you have done will not fade, it is too late
No one is going to ask for your daughter in marriage
You have already given her away.

Eli Oko

Until The Above

Hanging upside down in an empty room
Is the mannequin memory of the storyteller who never came back
Who bravely left land she knew to tell the tales of the few
And never found her way back

Sitting tied to a chair in a room, with a storm outside
Is the space holder who never knew how
Who slowly wandered far from her tribe, to serve those she felt
were in need
Only to find, the need in her was greater and far more consuming

Here in this small space that calls itself a home
Lies the Mother and Destroyer, the Nourisher and the Angel
of Death
Who came to be the contrasts in a world of light and shade
In a space of the loved and betrayed; to show us we are all we
dream ourselves to be

Here, now in this place of such stillness that even
Silence feels restless
Sat by a small fire is the frozen child of Hope
She came by this space, looking for warmth, to ease and thaw
her heart
And though the fire moves she is yet to learn that it is safe to sit
close by, she will not burn

And by the open window, by the branches of the trees that scrape
the pane
Are the guiding hands of so many who have come and gone in
this space
Who have landed and flown, who have gained and shall regain

Who will guide the child closer to the fire and show her she shall
not scald
Who will untie the damsel from her chair and show her freedom
Was not hers to give when not owned
Who will upturn the storyteller and remind her
No story can be honoured that has not been fed in us

Who will come and show this space the way to hold the many
faced shadows of the past
And who will walk through this all
Knowing we are all
And we are none of the above

Amber Agha

That Dreadful Eve

When I was but a little girl
a-sitting on me mother's knee
I dreamed of all the things I'd do,
the places I would go,
but then, one day, it dawned on me -
there's things they'll never let me be.

I might as well give up all hope;
sure they'll never let a girl be pope.
And I don't blame them, not at all,
sure wasn't it a woman who caused the fall.
Oh that dreadful Eve
from whose terrible sin
there'll be no reprieve.
Eternally divorced from God
We'll wander 'round on our tod -
the plight of all our sorry race
to be forever in disgrace.
'Twas all a woman's fault of course
on that finer point there'll be no recourse.

And after all what did she do?
When all is said and done -
She looked upon the tree of life, and thought
there must be more than being a wife.
She plucked an apple from the tree
thinking that's the very one for me.
And then the scales from her eyes did fall -
It wasn't a pretty site at all.

She looked at Adam standing there
and saw that he was bollocks bare.
Says she to him, you'd better have a bite -
I'll tell you now, it tasted shite.
But being a man and easily led
he did just what his woman said.

And then the voice of God was heard,
a rumbling from on high -
it was a scary thing, you know,
I'd not tell you a lie.
Says He to them, what have you done?
Says Eve to Adam, we'd better run.
And so they fled and went to bed
'Twas then that poor ol' God saw red.
Do you know what pissed Him off the most?
It wasn't the apple in her hand, oh no,
it was the fact that she could be so bold
and wouldn't do what she was told.
So there you have it, now you know
the reason why there is no hope -
they'll ever let a girl be pope.

Siobhan MacMahon

Match Of The Day

That old spangled bejellied bebangled slip of wellspring,
that old chaser time, a bag of tunes playing nerveless,
verveless, the elastic potential birdless, heat banging

in your chest,
something wriggling and giggling inside,
tick-tocking away beside,

and here's an old one who knows, sitting outside on the step,
on his porch, just taking it all in for a time, for a ride,
greenfinches, cats, the heliotropes all turning grateful bellies

to the yellow disc in the skies, their portraits, praying to Ra.

He's a cup o' brandyland in hand now
and as ever, pretending he's some old teahead
watching the sparring about to begin, as the cats sing out,

jealous, jealous eyes glowering about,
the dead will in their tickers at the bright birds
tuneful choir o' the greens, hearts bursting

with the blue sprung day, morning has spoken,
yellow light in the air and the picture book page
turns to patience

the skinny ones lapping and washing, bellies all raised to Ra,

the cats, watch, and wait,
as does the man on the step, only the hour of the clock
done with its darker hours sighed over, keeps steady tock,

the birds dart about at carolling and the cats' claws

flex, anticipatory, for an angle
from the bejangled skies to come crying down,

a feathered spiral and down,
down and falling, falling now, like dead souls right outta
the plain blue cry less skies

and up at them claws,
but the bird's teasing, they live free and high, diving again,
the sun rising higher and the cats call now, a draw, siesta.

Sarah Wallis

Breath Of Life

It's so new, the first intake
I can tell you don't like me
by your loud howl of protest
eyes screwed up, a fist of rage
all that time in the warm, dark
amniotic, umbilical, just when
you think you're safe, you're out!

Then you get used to me, you
take me for granted, that rise
and fall, absorbing me through
your skin, to you I'm just oxygen
fresh air wallpaper, outside space,
planets have their light, rain falls
clouds are dramatic, I'm invisible

but subtle, when I touch you like
a feathered wing, light, ultra cool
making leaves dance and tremble
carrying the scent of gardens after
rain, salt spray from the ocean
essence of memory, bittersweet
his face, her voice lingering on me.

Always there, in the black and blue
of your days, from whispered breeze
to gale-force warning, temper tantrum
rocking your cradle, singing lullabies
to you, warm, dark, in your favourite

place, hearing my voice, in those lonely
hours, against your windows and walls.

You may re-learn me, rediscover me
in quiet reflection, for an hour or so
now and then, but one thing's sure
like the last sad note of a saxophone
one day I'll leave you forever, escape
like a wisp of smoke, from your lips
like a cobweb pilgrim, vapour trail.

Here though, in this room, waiting
for me to fill your lungs like a sail
everything beginning for you, year
zero, as arms reach out, as you set
your face, and fist against me, after
all the trauma, you're here, because
of what I give. Life, and it's a miracle.

Nicola Wood

Teachers

For the ones whose backs I never saw
for the ones who talked in recipes
who could never spell and or pronounce my name
the ones who unpicked stems of daisies
who turned chains into dreamcatchers
for the one who referenced The Smiths at any given opportunity
for the ones with a light that never goes out
who wore energy like scarves
for the one who gave me antidisestablishmentarianism in my year
three spelling test
for the ones who wanted quiet
the ones who said I should speak more
who saw a thread of them in me
for the ones who chased mountain lions onto the playground to
give time for the goats to climb
for the traditional ones
for the ones with tattoos
who said fuck without apology
for the one with the bowl of oddly-shaped treasure
who actually made PowerPoints exciting
for the one with lightless eyes
who wore tortoise shell earrings and hid in them when fights
broke out
for the one with a belly full of water
who questioned everything
what do you want most from life
why haven't you used punctuation
why did you choose that word
what are you trying to say

why is your top button undone
where is your blazer
what scares you more than anything
do you want this life
are you willing to burn for it
for the ones who smiled often
the ones who knew what I needed
who had extra pens and built a ladder with them
for the one who said I would only get an A in maths
the one who was right
for the ones with soot under their nails
who bit into fireballs
as if they were apples
who told me I could do it too
for all of them
the one who stands before you is because of you

Charley Genever

Kiss From Above

I spy on androids
trading energy,
predictable business
diluting anger.
Dance of terminators
with victims and manipulators.

I hear cyborgs,
puppet-masters and automatons
in pre-recorded conversations,
toxic sleepwalkers
continuously accompanied by loops.
Sequence of submission
and infinite repetition.

History of resonance,
multilayered sound-scape
of contaminated consonants
and polluted syllables,
the soundtrack of the zombies
seems to have no end.

The monsters that robbed me,
the robots that envied me
the golems that sold me,
the demons that lighted the pyre.

Clans of cliché,
frightening and intimidating
heartless and unexciting,

sheepish and unaware.
Nightmare collective
of wolves in uniforms,
like troops raping out of boredom
or Nazis killing for sheer fun.

Labyrinth of bureaucrats
with no one to account for,
sound of excuses
but not a soul to blame
and nothing to avenge.

Dream of the damned
exceptionally defeated,
Joan and Guevara
Marley and Luxemburg,
Quichotte and Josephine
remembering justice
with no proof

but a kiss from above
travelling through the clouds,
continuously reshaping
into worlds of greater magnificence.
Awe and delight
foreshadowing forgiveness
and endless freedom.

Glorious tear
bursting with emotion,
dreaming of surrender
escape from ignorance,
all horror ever recorded.

Lucky me,
secret agent
in the war of sound.

Rosa Burgartz

Homeless (Sanctuary)

Suffering oak expel your pain,
Alone in your field with your desolate shame.
Once firmly rooted sturdy and grand
Beautifully serene like God's right hand.
A hand of sanctuary to all animal kind,
Nature's way of providing a social sturdy shrine.
Gracefully face your chainsaw death
Stripped of your forest your animals suppressed.
The last of the great oaks accept your fate
Scattered around the country under a thousand paperweights.

Anthony Robert Aked

The Woman I Was

I live with the memories of what I used to be.
Pondering.
My eyes are glossy and lit, bright as the sun can be.
My outer soul is dull, like the faint breath I still have.

My deep thoughts lie internally quiet.
My inner strength in my heart has gone,
the constant cruelty and terror takes my hope and will as its
reward;
embedding hate within my mind.
So conflicted and confused by my host.

My identity slowly peels away,
my self now more ghost like as the days go on.
I desperately cling onto memories of that innocent life I had,
a pain runs through me from head to toe;
grieving for what was once meant to be.

This women as pure as milk, has now gone, hidden.
Resolved, self-assured.
Will and life lost.
Cruelty often wins over my quiet timid ways,
always criticising, always abused by criticism.

Judgement and the weight of the world on my shoulders.
Am I to blame?
I try to love despite my rapid fall from grace,
caused by those who should have loved and protected me,
as I had loved them.

My eyes tear up as they reflect on this troubled soul.
I can and never will be whole again;
beaten and dragged down by life itself.
Everything that has happened has taken its toll.
The shell is now hollow and now I'm an outsider looking in.
Almost a corpse, part of the living dead.

How does my heart keep pumping and the blood run through my body?
Why do I still breathe?
How do I even know my name anymore?
I long for anyone and beg to be saved,
to help me be the woman I once was.

Natalie Verone Wilson

See Me

When you look at me, what do you see?
Am I a figment to some degree;
A mere construction of society;
A statistical minority?
Do you see who you think I should be,
Or is there a chance that perhaps you see me?

Am I a woman defined by her past,
Whose difference makes her a social outcast,
With a voice only as loud as the grave;
No more than a portrait that history engraved?
Do you see merely a daughter of slaves,
Or a heroine, strong, courageous and brave?

Do you see the struggles I have overcome,
My insurgent uprising from the slum?
Do you see the cage that entraps my dreams?
Can you hear the cries of my silent screams?
Do you see a martyr built of flesh and bone,
Or just that my skin does not match your own?

A legitimate child of Imperialism's seed,
I'm a by-product of a dissident breed
Whose ignorance wrought liberation's demise;
But freedom bought, with blood sacrificed.
From the soil of injustice grew indomitable will;
Though they slay my body, my spirit they can't kill.

Like a wounded soldier, I still battle on.
Conceived of my shame, my pride was born.

I'm not a model of social control.
I am a woman true to the depth of her soul.
I have an identity that is all my own,
And a passion so fierce, it sets fire to stone.

So, am I to you a modality;
A person defined by nationality;
A phantom of your mentality
Slotted into mass generality?
I ask again, what do you see?
If you open your eyes, you will see me.

Karen Francis

Mother Nature

My creator,
my bringer of life -
my Mother Nature.

You plucked me
From the ashes of euphoria.
You carried me
for three seasons,
Autumn, Winter and Spring.

You gave me life in the summer -
brought me into a world of light,
a world of warmth, filled with drumming hearts,
now with one more beat
joining the chorus of humanity.

Your face did not show your wisdom then,
your cheeks were blushed,
rivers of blood pooling in your cheeks.
Constellations of stars freckled your arms
Our universe on your skin.

Now, your skin is not as smooth,
but still beautiful.
The creases around your eyes
Are the valleys of our Rhônes-Alps.
They remind me of the good -
Of your laugh.

Your laugh. Oh, your laugh!
A clap of thunder,

filling the room not with fear,
but joy.

Your tears flood the valleys
around your eyes -
like a stream of melted snow
in the summertime.

Mother Nature, my love,
you needn't cry.

It can't be easy
Living with a storm -
a child who once was a dewy babe,
grown into devastation.

Hurricanes of anger,
rainy tears,
overcast depression littering your skies.
Flashes of lighting that attack you,
setting your world ablaze.
I'm sorry for being a storm.
I just hope you can remember

That after fire, after rain,
after bearing the storm,

Mother Nature continues to grow.
And so do you.

Izzi Seale

Believe In Your #Selfie

She hopped on the train
and slid in her seat,
clutching her bag,
ticket in her teeth,
rummaging for her phone
in the depths of her pocket,
in her 90's throwback denim jacket.

The W-Fi was down,
the journey was long,
sick of that Justin Bieber song
(oh come on - you know the one!
It was at number 1
for far too long!)
And like his refrain -
she'd heard again and again -
she took his advice whilst sat on that train
because she liked the way that she looked,
just as much
as that on point hook,
or that Hunger Games book,
so without mind or care for anyone else,
she began to love herself.

Selfie mode on,
cap pulled back,
phone on silent,
no click or flash:
head to the left

pout to the right -
the camera loved her in that light
alright.

She had a badass handle
on the tilt of that angle,
consumed by the lust
for the perfect lux,
she shot and re-shot,
cut and cropped,
lo-fi?
Nashville?
Oh, juno's hot!

An insta-ninja,
a hipster pinner,
a pouting, duck-lipped
00's grinner,
with unbeaten flair
for short hair
don't care,
with just a slight air
of 'oh, I've been there!'

And the 3 hours passed
in the quickest flash,
with no need to tag
and pit bull to red flag,
when the pic she loved most
she neglected to post,
and denied social media the honour to host.
'Cause she didn't need
her pose to bleed

its way onto your Facebook feed -
a like, a love, a viral fixation,
would never provide her true validation!

No, this girl had conviction,
knew it was healthy,
to believe in yourself,
sorry, to believe in your selfie!

Frankie Wilkinson

Silence

Just sit down and close your eyes
Stop and listen to the world outside
Can you hear that all around?
Listen carefully for the silent sound
In a world that never stops
We're missing out on quite a lot
Just for once, listen without speaking
Find out how the world is keeping
Appreciate the silence sound
For it speaks louder than all around
Some will find the peace and heal
For others the silence will feel unreal
But a powerful sound either way
One of which we need each day

Natalie Swain

The Biggest Liar

I step on the scales -
Waves through my feet like an electric shock
My eyes bulge out in surprise at the unexpected, must-be-
corrected number...

The scales are broken.
It is the obvious conclusion or a delusion
Perhaps.
I go to the gym, I spin, I am thin.
Aren't I?
I do circuits, abs, squats, I run
never for fun.
My bum may be a bit plump but
it's the muscles.
I'm no longer in my twenties, my hips must have grown
Larger, curvier, softer... wider?

I know - too much water, or vegetables, or soup
That must be why I bloat!
I swallow a weepy note in my throat, the pain for such hated
weight gain.
It's stress - that's why I no longer fit in my dress; too much
caffeine creates
bum extension and water retention.
I need a cleanse.
Fennel, Melissa, psyllium, nettles, dandelion, peppermint, red
clover, ground ivy
Disgusting!
But I drink, I swallow, I brew in the morning, in the day, in the
evening

Cleansing and detoxing, detoxing and cleaning.

I look better, thinner, slimmer, my skin shimmers but
Alas! The hated number doesn't decrease but it's increased!
Please call Greenpeace!
I am a whale, a walrus, a sea lion
I see blubber, flab and fat rolls!
Liars! The scales are wrong; how can I be so out of control?

So I sit and cry, I hate the lying scales
I hate myself, my body; I'm enraged, outraged;
I change the batteries. Nothing changes.
So I sit and cry and wonder who is
The biggest liar.

Teresa Lari Long

Untitled

I drift discarded wood
Along the shoals abreast the waves
The current soothes a cradle
As she rocks my sodden grave

Warm holiday shores
Wherein you laughed and frolicked with delight
Are jagged with neglect
Which led to death for we that night

Suspended in a seaside womb
Drowned herein a watery tomb
I am the child a world forgot
I am the child you left to rot

You chose to let my family die
The day you chose to close your eyes
- To war-torn, gambit refugees
Because you found no place for we

As your humanity subsides
Another child of Syria dies
The azure sky burns shamefaced red
For all the blood of Syria's dead

Our only crime? To flee a life
Where bombs and bullets rain from sky
And savage rapings of our mother
Or brutal beatings of our brothers

Mean that we're the lucky ones
Because that day we are not harmed

Procrastination of salvation
And your tabloid education
Has suppressed our desperate voice
Leaving we with but one choice

Have faith to brave the treacherous seas
In cargo holds or cramped dinghies
And pray to God his sympathy
Survive, or die with dignity

But can you see me now?
Now salted water fills my lungs
And do you hear me now?
Now that the sea has ceased my tongue

And can you see me now?
That I lay washed up on your beach
And will you hear us now?
My haunted voice for Syria pleads.

Helen Mather Rogers

To All Tea Drinkers

To all tea drinkers

Better than that,
better than some Facebook friendship
unfriended by wit of disrespecting
my sister, than tripping
the jerk who took out
my legs on the edge of the area,
better than withholding the tax
from a council who don't take my bins,
than giving the finger
to the man in the red car
who cut me up
at the lights, I am better
than kicking the lights out
of the man who cut up my sister,
than withholding the life
of the man who took off my leg
with an axe on the edge of his area,
than beating to death the man
from the council who stole
my tax to buy his red car,
than cutting the face off the wit
who jerked my sister, the man who pointed
his finger, who stood on my bins
still on my face,
though I could see nothing
but the blackness of blood,
I felt him go down, heard them

chanting my name, I'm better than that.
I am changing the man who came to kill,
the man who loves
his cows and his brothers, who drives
a red car, I know this man,
I stare at his face until it is mine,
he called me his brother, picked me out
from the amputation queue,
saved from the blackness
of blood, the beating to death,
I drank tea with the raped
and the maimed, drank tea
with the rapist and the machete men
when they chanted my name.
To all tea drinkers, I raise my
pen, I stare at your faces until
they are mine. I once drove a red car,
saw nothing but the
blackness of blood.

Ken Sullivan

Ashes To Ashes

Ash.
The ash tree. Softly, gently sways
from side to side. Across the garden fence,
arms outstretched, never quite
reaching the greener grass.
Freshly cut. The scent burns
my senses, reminding me
of home.

Home.
The pleasant smiles
between father and daughter. Returning
from school to a hand-cooked meal,
made from scratch. The cats
can smell the meat. They pounce
and stop to gently nudge
my face.

Face,
my fears. Height is
one. Just one branch at a time.
It isn't an essence, you have all day, night
can wait. Then I can rest my weary head
on my pillow while the sandman comes.
Dreaming, sleep allowing
my growth.

Growth,
the apple trees
at the back of the garden. Growing

ever taller, wider, over the barrier.
Into neighbouring enemy grounds. Bearing gifts
to all men, to be harvested
as the fruits of peace,
not war.

War.
My mother and father,
father and grandmother. The cycle
fights never ending, in a living hell. The torment
of an evil soul, no rest. For wicked
I have been, but 'tis no good to dwell on matters past,
for that is where they burn and turn
to ash.

Ash.
The tree is gone,
now. My father with it. My old,
life beginning anew. Everyone deserves a new
start. We have one book, but many chapters. Fragments
piece together to form our lifeline. The end of one,
is the beginning of the next.
and from the ashes,
we rise.

India D'Vaz

Girl

I see this little
long haired blonde girl
Getting her nails done
in a beauty salon
By this long haired brunette
with talons
and a 'tan'.
This woman has so much make-up on
She has become a caricature of everything that's wrong
With modern concepts of beauty,
Blinded by her thick fake lashes
She lives in a bubble she cannot see.
Her salon bright pink, covered in glitter and littered with spelling
mistakes.
This little long haired blonde girl;
Just a small child
Who should be out playing, exploring, getting dirt under those
nails
Gazes out of the window in boredom,
I walk past on the outside
Her eyes
Analyze my short hair
My bright dress
And she looks half confused
Half... impressed
As though she were relieved
to finally see something different,
to see another colour other than the sea of orange
On which she has been swept without consent into the current

To see she doesn't have to follow the prescription
Of the beauticians recommendations
Manifestations of flaws
That are actually her imprint
Her unique fingerprint
I can see as I smile at her eyes
She is thinking
She feels different
But her lungs are filled with overpowering perfume
And her mind is filled with poison
Perpetuated in her mums celebrity magazines
and papers.
It's like
the juxtaposition of the beautician
And the poet
Illuminated something within her
Some sort of... development,
and as I walk past
I hope she won't succumb to the indifference
Of the herd
Just another camouflaged
with manicures and extended hair
I hope she learns
Before it's too late,
I hope she doesn't except her fate.

Gemma Baker

Compass Points

Scratched into the desk; names of the future,
pre-echoes of the shape of things to come,
scrawled with newly acquired compass points,
a fresh pair every Autumn term,
the poorer kids used blunt cast-offs.

We know that Kilroy was here,
along with unsavoury young ladies
of less exacting standards; fictitious of course,
merely figments of the boys' dreams,
each scholar, a product of the system,
would run a cross-country mile
if they ever met a girl in the flesh,
stunted development, socially awkward,
they learned their Latin lines
telling dirty jokes about Canuleia,
hoping that a Plebeian girl
would never be their lot,
unless it was a village lass for a quick fumble.

They scribbled letters home to parents
which were mandatory like cold showers,
passing the time on wet Sunday afternoons.

Time capsules, secret messages to the future,
each generation left their mark,
every good boy explored intricacies in the fretwork,
imagining his hands explored nether regions,
down in the valley, where nobody knows.

The Bursar contemplates sanding them down,
purging the parchment, hiding the hieroglyphics,
a Rosetta stone bereft of a private key,
publicly the school treats it as history
while counting millennia in battles and boys,
so many lost to the Great War,
their pain goes back before the Crimea,
such a shame to destroy all those incantations,
in the end, the desks survive as silent messengers.

Dave Brooks

Umbrella Prophet

It was the 7:26, not my normal train.
You all crammed on at Watford / Bushey / Harrow
and more with each stop. I didn't look up,
let alone get up, in case my seating loss
became another arse's gain.
You were pregnant. I know that now,
but honestly I wasn't sure at first.
And though unmoving rudeness is poor form,
accusations false have proven worse.
A few stops further on of sweating human crush
we stopped (at Shepherd's Bush?), and somewhere far away
a flicker registered on seismic charts:
tectonic plates of people straining to depart.
'Wait!' you called as punters grinded past.
They slowed just for a second, didn't dare engage
with you, a crazy yeller,
waving an umbrella.
I saw its owner.
He looked at you a little longer than the rest,
but off the train already there's no way
for him to fight back on, and anyway
the queues behind the ticket gates were growing.
He glanced at the umbrella knowing
price of everything, value of nothing:
he could get another from his company
so barely broke his stride.
And then I looked and saw your eyes
pleading with a base intensity

as if you knew the umbrella's the way
of saving its now former owner from his destiny.
I won't forget those livid green and shining eyes.
Umbrella Prophet waving your stone tablet,
but finding no belief with London Midland's heathens.
When you sat down something within those eyes
had not quite died, but had been put away.
You had joined us.
You sat in silence all the rest of the way.
I turned back to my Kindle
and glowered at the liquid crystal.

T L Evans

Hope

Don't talk to me of man and gun,
How heroes stand and cowards run,
Don't talk to me of bombs that thud,
When hill and vale runs red with blood,
Don't talk to me of lands and rights,
When bargaining down rifle sights,
Don't talk to me of cannons' roar,
When to me they all mean war.

Don't talk to me of man and gold,
When people starve both young and old,
Don't talk to me of planes and cars,
When people sleep beneath the stars,
Don't talk to me of styles of hair,
When children walk with feet so bare,
Don't talk to me of who shall lead,
When to me they all mean greed,

Don't talk to me of stocks and shares,
When one mistake can cost careers,
Don't talk to me of merchandise,
When children work for a bowl of rice,
Don't talk to me of independent rule,
When ethnic cleansing is unjust and cruel,
Don't talk to me of persecution,
When to me it means execution,

Don't talk to me of race and creed,
When any colour of skin if cut does bleed,
Don't talk to me of holy wars,

When the innocent die because of cause,
Don't talk to me of religious zeal
When people get killed for faith and ideal
Don't talk to me of self-sacrifice,
When once a martyr meant something nice

But talk to me of family love,
Of your Lord God and Heaven above,
And talk to me of how to trust,
The confidence to share one's crust,
And talk to me of peace on land,
With fellow man hand in hand,
And talk to me of how to cope,
When to me it all means hope.

Bazil Figura

European

I am a European.
Voted to remain in its union, but
tragically when it came to ballot,
there were too few kindred spirits damn it.
But 48% does not make us dissident.
Just meant that we are intent on the future of our children
and our children's children, not being bent out of shape like some
discarded old leather.
To safeguard, protect, assure that life can be better.

I am a European.
My veins flow with the blood of Britain and France,
and I didn't leaflet and campaign to remain
for Farage to slash my heritage like a boil to be lanced.
Didn't fall for his merry dance, scoffing lies in a tanked-up trance.

I am a European.
Yes, political logic bolstered my reasons for remaining,
I won't go into details, I'm just saying;
But this is my identity, so I don't appreciate the retorts about
'Brexit, just accept it, respect it',
because Europe is my chemistry and mentally this has affected
me.

I am a European.
Myself and England will always be so geographically,
but England's influence will be reduced drastically and rapidly with
a people less tolerant and educated culturally.
And next year if François Hollande is not shunned,
and France decide they are also through with the EU,

France will still be continental, the result more politically incidental,
The rupturing more gentle...

I am a European.

Sigrid Marceau

When I Say I Miss You, This Is What I Mean

When I say I miss you this is what I mean:
There's this dread, it's like you're dead, like you love someone else instead,
I'm fed up of not knowing and that's owing to your silence...

And the distance, some kind of resistance.

This distance, it's a circumstance we have to live with, get to grips with,
But will we ever live with one another, more than sister/brother,
Will we ever wed, share the same bed, love each other 'til we're dead?
Will we be married, carried off into the sunset where we met? I'm so quick to forget
How it felt, how you made my heart melt like the wax of the candle that's going out,
Because we aren't, and I don't know what this is anymore,
If it's some kind of chore or if it has love at its core,
Because what I can't ignore is that it makes my heart sore just thinking about you.

So why don't you get off the fence, stop making it so tense?
It doesn't make sense, we could be immense.

You don't deserve this, being put on the reserve list,
You used to be on the wish list, the take-the-risk list,
When we first kissed, the this-is-it list.

The truth is I miss you,
Can't resist you when I'm with you

But you're not here and all I can hear when you're not near
Is your silence.

Rebekah Vince

Dark Angel

A latent thought in cloying dark
The crossroads with a question mark
The hesitation undefined
The anger of unbalanced minds
Who to turn to, where to go
The evil one will surely know
The voice whilst sinking in the sand
As Dark Angel takes you by the hand

One more she cries as she pulls you free
One more soul for my Lord to be
Rich pickings from an evil world
Man or woman, boy or girl
It doesn't matter much to me
Hell's fires burn bright their destiny
Too late to cry out to be saved
Your soul lies in an unmarked grave

Through caves and tunnels underground
The screams, the cries, the haunting sounds
Echoes of those passed before
Too late to go back through the door
A portal to an unknown place
Here on this world now taking place
Beware the thought that's in your mind
Dark Angel isn't far behind

Through the burning fires of eternal Hell
And the molten metal wishing wells
To the cemetery of burnt-out souls

Where through evil thoughts did each enrol
Beware the road that leads to night
Stay focused on God's holy light
Look out for crossroads and for sand
And never take Dark Angel's hand

For one latent thought in cloying dark
Brings a crossroad with a question mark
And the voice whilst sinking in the sand
As Dark Angel takes you by the hand and...

Keith Nuhrenburg-Wilson

Fearless

Life's journey is treacherous,
every being having a purpose,
of sacrifice and success,
our consistent belief is the true test.
To know our own way,
is not for us to say,
to map out our future,
only prevents the great adventure,
to fear failure,
overexposes us to feel no pleasure,
to not climb our mountains,
in pain, we would remain.
Having a dream gives you ambition,
courage is fighting its mission,
to believe allows you to achieve,
which is anything but naive,
for life is too short,
for one's attitude to not support.
Go forward with gumption,
do not believe one's assumption,
for minds so small,
only comprehend the awaiting fall.
No one can foresee,
if it is meant to be,
but to not even try,
you'll forever ask why?
Take the plunge into life's unknown,
to follow you'll only be a clone.

Buy the ticket,
to witness the final wicket,
aboard that plane,
though to some it seems insane,
dance in the rain,
in your best attire up the lane,
wholehearted expression gives you fame.
In your life be sometimes reckless,
but not completely careless,
I believe to be fulfilled,
you must be fearless.
This doesn't mean having no fears,
or holding back tears,
but in spite of doubt,
or lurking frights,
we chose to always fly that kite.

Megan Dodson

1916

I find a soldier's ration tin,

entrenched, submissively,

in the mud.

Opening it,

I look for a disembodied memory.

But I do not hear the

staccato exchange

of bullets across wide,

empty plains.

No sound of shrill whistles

blowing across the Western Front.

I won't know his dexterity when

holding a rifle,

how sensation was measured

by the broken skin on his

frostbitten feet.

The clenching of his stomach

as he stared into the writhing whites

of shouting boys,

up to their necks in mud.

Mad boys,

having watched bodies upon bodies contort

and pupate.

Would his family recognise him

with shell-shocked earth clinging to his body?

I can't read his letters,

perhaps complimenting his loved one

for sending him a useful rag.

How, on this day

he used it as a tablecloth,

a bed sheet,

a dressing,

a shroud.

Stephen Foot

Your Final Journey

At an early age I learnt the true value of a grandad
And ever since that day I have treasured every second with you
Every smile, every laugh and every tear created precious memories
Our bond grew stronger than most and will withstand the depths
of time

I always knew that one day our time in this realm would come to
an end
But I couldn't comprehend just how strong the heartache would
be
My entire being is writhing and screaming from the pain
The void from your absence is never-ending, and I ask myself can
it ever heal?

I know another dimension exists where one day we will meet
again
But please Grandad while we do wait, can I ask you to do this for
me?
Come and visit me, my door will never close for you
Let me know you are okay and at peace, and that my love for you
shines bright

All I have left now are my thoughts of times gone by
These will remain engraved into my heart for all eternity
They will travel with me wherever I may go
And in time I hope to be able to reminisce and smile rather than
cry

I hope that you are now resting, with no more pain and suffering
Do not feel sorrow and miss us, for we shall all rejoin together one
day

And never forget just how much you mean to me

But now the time has come to say goodbye while you embark on your Final Journey

Kayleigh Cottrell

Songbird

What does the songbird sing?
Does it sing of the places it's never been?
The way it gets to move daily, yet never flying free,
Or, does it sing of things it's never seen,
Where winds blew it back, to keep it where be,
Oh songbird, sing your blues to me...

The poor little songbird,
It's always heard but never understood,
Alone in the night-time,
In the darkness of a thorn branches wood,
Too afraid to sing and be heard,
Like the little songbird should.

The autumn was ever occurring by now,
Summer sweet memories now an autumn decaying day,
By nature, the season was taking as much as it could,
The songbird would wake one day,
To find its home furthermore, blown away,
In the loss of the crimson leaves and aged trees,
The songbird will sing while it journeys to a new day.

The days and nights gone by,
The nights have grown too cold,
The little songbird has left and felt forced to move on,
Its songs of summer have now played old,
Just like a record we all used to know,
The whistling, if you listen closely,
It can still be heard around the tree,

of which the little song bird used to be,
You hear it in memory of beauty,
I feel it was left behind, just for you and me.

Daniel Link

On White Horse Hill

In the belly of the dragon-horse I sit,
its white spine arching over me
one fluid curve running
from the forgotten to the unknown.
Here, in the sunlit now,
I hug my knees to my heart
tell my sorrows to the wind.
The words are pulled from my lips
shredded and spun
into filaments
for the crows to swing upon.

Below me the earth falls away
into folds and furrows,
waves and undulations.
Tiny sheep feed in the hollow.
Tiny people pass in tiny cars;
tiny lives moving from breath to breath
and blurring at last into blue distance and shadows.

I hold on,
fingers clawed knuckle-deep in the muddy ground
watching
until cold and responsibilities force movement from me.

I uncurl,
turn again
to the world of solicitors and wills
insurance evaluations and sombre conversations;
the cracked filler of bureaucratic practicalities

inadequately masking the sucking hole
that her death
has kicked
in my life.

I leave,
and as I pass
the skylarks rise up singing.
The notes drift from the greying sky
like snow,
settle briefly on my hunched shoulders
in a cooling balm
of temporary serenity.

Kat Lyons

Gaia Exposed

Beneath our feet her heart's core pulses,
shaping time itself around each tiny beat of life.
The acorn sprouts.
The bulbs set forth their questing shoots to find the sunshine,
drinking in each ray with thirsty need,
their greed outweighing
forms so slender as to bend or break if tousled by a breeze's
softest kiss.

She nurtures all.

And in her mother's love we each lay blessed.
As mountains rise to tower over valleys filled with floral sculpture,
life takes wing with songs to echo through the seasons,
meant to fill even the coldest hearts with joy.

If only we could see her pain.

As with each passing year her assets stripped and bared
by all consuming greed we bleed her dry.

Raped.

Despoiled.

Her bubbling streams of tears becoming
torrents in a hopeless bid to wash away the grief and shame.

She was our world.

Yet in the rush of life it seems that she has been forgot,
And soon her vital heart will cool and harden,
leaving just a barren star to hang suspended and unwanted
in the galaxy with all our broken dreams.

Cassie Hughes

Sunrise Of Life

I profoundly desire the sun's light;
beatific, half-sloped and rising
from its intimate bed of dreams -
and when fully awake and round,
shining inspiration on dreams.

Window's cobwebs gleaming threads
like halos not yet fully skeined
offer delicate strength in the face
of dawn's vast luminescent wings.

That living radiance is hope and wonder,
supremely incandescent, as though life
is grander than it seemed.

Then heading back to bed,
the majestic silent body
lowering its florescent knowledge
into the realm of finished psalms
of careful, darkened sleep
that plans its next awakening.

To be deprived of witnessing
this awesome orb releasing power
and vivid blooms, its ability to thrive
and grow and orchestrate our lives,
to gaze and weep with gratitude
for everything denied during hours
of dark and mindless sleep
would be the death of love for light

So yes, I must be there
to watch that awesome sun arise
and speak to everything that knows
where life begins. I too must feel
the pulse of solar generosity as precious art.

Karen Eberhardt-Shelton

Do You See?

Did you see the picture of the swollen-bellied child,
Beset with flies nobody had the strength to brush away?
Did you see his mother, as weak as he is,
Whose one remaining hope is that he dies first;
Not to be left to die alone?
Have you seen the water hole,
Shared by incontinent wildlife,
Where they are forced to drink each day?
Who cares?
The aid worker cares,
Risking health and sanity,
Trying to stem the tide of human suffering
While supplies dwindle.

Did you see the pictures of the latest fighter plane?
One hundred million pounds a time.
The government's ordered eight.
Eight hundred million pounds, available it seems,
To kill people.
What price saving some?
Who cares?

The child doesn't react to the sonic boom above.
Only the flies panic and briefly leave him

Did you see those pictures of the other side of Mars?
Have you seen the budget for man's never-ending quest
To understand the galaxy and the origin of stars?
Who cares about the origin of stars?

The child with distended belly and flies on his eyes,
Will not see the other side of tonight.
Who cares what's on the other side of Mars?
Who cares?

Bryn Strudwick

Bonds

Sam swelled with pride the day she arrived -
A tiny bundle with her mother's eyes
to change his life,
shift his focus from himself
to this miraculous slice of boundless wealth,
no one more surprised at the transformation
of the shape his world would take
as he sampled the delights of a newborn child.

This was something unexpected,
new adventures to be enacted
and a lifestyle unforeseen,
a clean break from a troubled past
a golden chance to atone at last
for the corridor of pain
forever encasing the family name

This was fresh -
The intense heat of a humid week
fanned with dreams and expectations,
renewed relations with hope and aspirations.
Things were going to be different now,
this beautiful gift a magic wand
already conjuring incredible bonds,
creating stepping stones to future days
when she would have it so much better
in innumerable ways,
than it had ever been for him
as he followed the language of love to the letter

Letting
Olivia
Victoria's
Existence

be his sole reason for living.

Clive Oseman

Let's Storm The Night

Last night I made a paper moon
And placed it in the sky above your head.
Fabric clouds; tumbling sheets of night -
Let's paint the town red.
The stars I made from glitter too:
Studs of shivering silver;
They twinkle just like your eyes do
And make the trees quiver.

I'll hold the words,
Then you'll hold the pictures,
That fall from a velvet brush.

We've stolen the show,
As everyone sleeps:
Dreaming of things like money and clothes -
Which is silly.

You just close your eyes like me
And something's there;
Lay down on the blanket of grass
That's ours,
Staring up at the world
We created.

Let's storm the night,
Chase the skies into dawn;
Their misty shades and orange hues
At your command.

Draw a pastel sun from your fingertips
And forge the streets with clay.
We'll run right down them,
Leaving our footprints behind -
A tracing, so clear;
Yet no one will know,
That we were ever there.

Victoria McAnerney

Mohamedou's Release

(Released from Guantanamo 17th October 2016)

Almost fifteen years of unbridled hell
Scandalous tortures, still you survive
Using fortitude, courage, humanity, strength
Bury scars deeply, rejoice, you're alive.

A new beginning...

The joy of life unfolding free
Each day an unplanned gift
Comfort, peace, with rest assured
Consolidation time to drift

Pleasures of the years to come
Moments unending new to explore
Slow to rise, late mornings awakening
Life to be lived as never before

A space renewed to freely breathe
Forgotten memories retrieved
The beauty of autumn's golden trees
Pathways steeped in amber leaves

The freshness of a morning spills
On shaded mountain's frosted gowns
Where sleepy villages their spires
Stand resolute and peace abounds

Nature nurtures, her calming touch
Timeless healing making whole
An enigma of calm in driving storm
An aphrodisiac, feeding the soul.

Susan Erskine

6am

6am on a train heading north
Steel Titans holding up the sky
Atlas reincarnated
Ancient gods raising the earth from slumber
An ice-blue sunrise full of potential
A white-gold sky full of heartbreak
Endless forests and giants of stone
Empty carriages and empty hearts
6:45 on a train heading north

7pm on a train heading south
Gods of stone overpower steel titans
The sky in shades of plum and violet
Lush forests
Persephone returned
Rolling hills clear skylines
The damming curve of her lips
Curled into a smile
A final moment of peace
A mirror of the mountains in the distance
7:04 on a train heading south

11pm on a train heading north
Steel Titans remain
Stars are like diamonds scattered across velvet
Past the smog
A yellow night

The streets lined with ghosts of good memories
An echo of a confession on the lips of the damned
11:32 on a train heading north

Maeve Moon

Dropping Anchor

Indigenous, inbred
In this blue planet;
Through conception to birth,
Metamorphosed.
Confined, constrained
In flesh and blood.

Untethered soul
Begs question
Who can I be?
I am who I am.
With truth revealed
My eyes have seen.

Privily pass through
Invisible veil
To beauty and glory
From this cosmic jail,
Where the key
Belongs to he
Who would prevent
The Love that Is.

Love that powers
The universe:
Its gentle strength
Devours hate.
Pride takes a fall:
Foiled ego trips,

That highlight self
In silver lips.

The light of grace
Streams through the haze,
Exposing cracks
Of dreary days.
Superficiality...
Crumbles...
In its glory.

Beryl Jupp

Crash

And twisted metal shards of glass
and twisted metal shards of glass
and nothing ever seems to last
apart from you.
A slowly sinking pit of dread
it hurts my head to think you're dead
and never more frequent my bed
content to dream of you instead
as dreams are things that last forever.
And twisted metal shards of glass
and twisted metal shards of glass
Darkened roadside
lit by glint of headlight beam
a quiet scene
or so it seemed
but I did not witness horror vision
as I sat at home with television
on
film reflecting harsh reality
as I raced to the scene
my thoughts unclean
with fright in flight
held back tonight
to see you sitting
then hold you tight
just you
just me

just pale moonlight
and so survived
to continue our lives
again.

Andrew Nicholls

Sacred Journey

Fate is the road
That begins at birth;
The route is straight
And lined with fences;
The human race, in
Single file, must
Climb the hills and
Cross the bridges;
Until we reach the
Point of death, where
The body dies, but
The soul is saved;
Its destination
Is preordained.

David Mobberley

Untitled

I walked through the doorway to watch them bring you back to
life.
I thought that you would make it,
but that was the last time I saw your face alive.
The ambulance took your body far away from home.
If I had known this was the end I would have told you so much
more.
My sky is falling tonight.

Morgan Welsh

FORWARD POETRY INFORMATION

We hope you have enjoyed reading this book - and that you will continue to enjoy it in the coming years.

For free poetry workshops please visit
www.forwardpoetry.co.uk.
Here you can also join our online writing community 'FP Social' and subscribe to our monthly newsletter.

Alternatively, if you would like to order further copies of this book or any of our other titles, then please give us a call or log onto our website.

Forward Poetry
Remus House
Coltsfoot Drive
Peterborough
PE2 9BF

(01733) 890099